YOUNG PLAYWRIGHTS FOR CHANGE

an anti-bullying play anthology

Theatre for Young Audiences/USA
American Alliance for Theatre & Education

2013–14

Michael A. Van Kerckhove and Jeff Jenkins, Editors
Book Design by Larry Kozial at Makeworks (makeworks.co)
Cover Illustration by Borja Cabada (bonesandsmithereens.com)

Theatre for Young Audiences/USA, Chicago, Illinois
American Alliance for Theatre & Education, Bethesda, Maryland

YOUNG
PLAYWRIGHTS
FOR CHANGE

USA/ASSITEJ

Comments: Email publications@tyausa.org.

Note: Biographical information pertains to the 2013–14 academic year.

Published by:

Theatre for Young Audiences/USA
c/o The Theatre School
2350 N. Racine Ave.
Chicago, IL 60614
tyausa.org
info@tyausa.org

American Alliance for Theatre & Education
4908 Auburn Ave.
Bethesda, MD 20814
aate.com

Library of Congress Control Number: 2015951293

ISBN 978-0-9966008-0-4

Table of Contents

* National Contest Winner
** National Contest Runner-Up

Foreword

By Stan Foote, Artistic Director,
Oregon Children's Theatre,
Portland, Oregon

Andrew & Nita,

With your help,
ripples of change!

In sociology, the Ripple Effect addresses how social interactions can affect situations not directly related to the initial interaction. Throw a pebble into water and it will make a ripple. Those ripples interact with their environment and create small changes to that environment. Increase the number of pebbles and you increase the number of ripples.

The goal of Young Playwrights for Change is to amplify the voices of young playwrights and to spark meaningful conversations about the topic of bullying throughout classrooms, schools, and communities. We hope to create energy that will ripple across our nation to provoke thought, discussion, and change.

The first ripple was created by a phone conversation between Michael Bobbitt, Producing Artistic Director of the Adventure Theatre in Maryland, and me. We were both proud board members of Theater for Young Audiences, USA (TYA/USA). We asked each other a series of questions: How do we help kids who are being bullied? What happens if professional theaters from around the country joined forces to address the bullying epidemic? Could we make an impact?

Several weeks later our fellow board members joined us on this quest. We also joined forces with the American Alliance for Theatre and Education (AATE). The organizations pledged a three year focus on bullying. They encouraged members to write plays, share work and workshops on the topic.

Michael Bobbitt started a local playwriting contest for middle school students. He asked the kids to write ten-minute plays on the topic of bullying. It was a brilliant idea! Give voice to the young people who are affected daily by bullying. Seventeen young playwrights submitted their work. They received mentorship from professional playwrights. They discussed their plays with teachers, peers, and family. Michael even toured three of the plays to schools in the area.

I asked Michael if Oregon Children's Theatre (OCT) could replicate his project. We did, and were thrilled with the response. OCT received sixty-five entries for the Bully Project. Many were classroom projects, with stacks of plays being delivered within minutes of the deadline. Six finalists were selected and mentored by professional playwrights. OCT hosted staged readings of the plays. One of the plays was produced at the young playwright's school. All of this caused more discussion about the topic that rippled throughout our community.

Around the same time, I spoke with Karen Sharp, Education Director at Seattle Children's Theatre and President of Theatre for Young Audiences/USA (TYA), and we discussed taking the Bully Project to a national audience. TYA joined forces with the American Alliance of Theatre and Education to create a national contest.

Two hundred forty-seven plays were entered into local, regional, and the national competition. Each one of those young playwrights started their own ripples by talking with friends, parents, and teachers about their plays. Many were performed in classrooms. Thousands and thousands of conversations were generated and the ripple effect is in full motion.

And here we are, with an incredible anthology of fourteen plays written by young people for young people. My wish is that they are performed and discussed in classrooms around the country so they may continue causing ripples of change.

Introduction

by Mary Hall Surface, Artistic Director,
INTERSECTIONS Festival at
Atlas Performing Arts Center,
Washington, DC

Everyone can remember a time when someone said something that hurt your feelings, just to get a laugh or attention from others. What about the time when you were excluded, intentionally, from a group or a game? Or the time you stood by when someone else was called names? Teasing, taunting, pushing, and shoving remain in our memories, whether it happened decades ago or yesterday. Happily, schools nationwide are actively confronting these behaviors and working to create cultures built on kindness and inclusion rather than on power and intimidation. But as the young playwrights in this collection reveal, bullying in its many forms is all too alive and well in school hallways, on playgrounds, and in families. These short plays are sharp windows into the world of bullies and the bullied, imagined by fourteen middle school playwrights who have turned their talents toward exploring this pervasive social dynamic.

Fueled by workshops on the local and regional levels, these young playwrights have harnessed their imaginations to create places that are achingly real, as well as wildly imaginative. From living rooms to classrooms to fantasylands, the settings provide diverse characters places to discover who they want to be and how they want to live. Each play is rich with performance opportunities for young actors who like to delve into complex characters. Indeed, a consistent theme throughout the plays is that people, even bullies, are rarely one-dimensional. Directors will enjoy discovering ways to capture the cinematic style of many of the plays, which change time and place as rapidly as a social media news feed. At ten minutes long, each play is an ideal catalyst for class or club discussion or, even better, as the centerpiece of a school assembly or community meeting designed to take an honest look at middle school culture.

The top prize-winning play spotlights how theatre can use comedy to spotlight a serious subject. Michael Ford's *Nerdy Nate and the Anti-Bullying Quest* presents a wonderfully fun spin on a tale of a nerd-turned-hero, his loyal sidekick, and the dreaded bully-villain. Super-hero comics, whacky video games, and good ole-fashioned melodrama inspire the playful plot and broad characters. This imaginative romp offers a delightful "sword of confidence" against bullying through smart silliness and some great surprises. All roles can be played by either gender, making it especially flexible and appealing for production.

Chloe Rust's *Bullies Anonymous*, the national runner-up, takes us inside a quirky, unusual recovery group, convened by a former bully for the purpose of rehabilitating a group of less-than-eager participants. One character is the nasty-gossip-gone-viral — the cyber-bully. By giving us a chance to see the spiraling exchanges among a group where each is accustomed to being at the top of the power pyramid, Chloe unravels some of the "whys" of these well-drawn characters and offers just a taste of how they might change.

While all of the plays look at characters making choices in difficult circumstances, several highlight the individual courage required when faced with bullying. In Darci Ramirez's *Combo Pizza*, a teen invites her friends into a new way of thinking, inspired by her brother who is disabled. Rather than antagonize people who are different, why not strive to see what is distinctive and interesting about them? In Eugenia Montsaroff's *The New Girl*, a curious new student reaches out to the class bully to surprising results. In Riley Ellis's *You Are Not Alone* we meet a teen that turns near-tragedy into an empowering product. She creates a documentary that includes an interview with the girl who verbally abused her younger sister. Paige Wolf's *Can't Let Go* looks at a girl's steadfast loyalty to a friend in the midst of hurtful competing-for-a-boyfriend behavior. The difference one person can make is very clear in these dramas.

A collective response to bullying centers Anna Lomsadze's *A Little Push*. Here a spunky new student unites his friends against the long-feared school nemesis. In Joshua Curry's *Founding's Day*, two cousins, one from a tribe of outcasts, take an extraordinary step in the face of hostile behavior stoked by prejudice. This powerful play reveals how theatre can probe contemporary issues by setting them in future or imagined worlds.

How to involve adults in confronting bullying shapes the plot of several plays. In Sophie Nicholson's *A Tale of Two Bullies*, a middle school girl asks her teacher to support her in standing up to two friends who are bullying a new student. In Ibrahim M. Sillah's *Getting Past the Radar*, two boys struggle with wanting to report a bully, but not wanting to be "tattlers." Both plays take a hard look at the importance and the challenge of reaching out to trusted adults.

Adults play very different roles in other plays. Claire M. Edwards' *Math Behind Amusement Parks* shows how a boy is hurtfully imitating the behavior of his bullying father. MJ Stone's *Project: Bully* offers sympathetic insight into the conflicted feelings of a bullied-at-home boy who wants to change his behavior at school, but is afraid to lose his status. In Daniel Madigan's *Uncouth Substitute*, a boy finally reaches out to the principal for help and then meets the mother of his tormentor – an equally bullying teacher. Neglectful parents are the source of a girl's aggression in Bergen Haggart's *Dani's Story*. While not excusing the behavior, this revelation helps Dani understand why the bullying is happening and, more importantly, that it is not her fault. As the character Elmer from *You Are Not Alone* says: "... you don't need to change yourself. You are not the problem, the bullies are. And, it will get better."

As a judge of the national contest that selected these plays, I am excited by their potential to impact both the making of theatre that matters and the raising of awareness that is essential. May all these plays be a window into a world getting better.

SCRIPT 1

Nerdy Nate and the Anti-Bullying Quest

By Michael Ford

Characters (each can be played by a boy or girl):

Nerdy Nate / Natalie – Confident, but a bit reserved and dorky

Fraidy Fred / Francine – Nate's best friend, somewhat stuttery and shy

Prince / Princess Mirrorgaze – Self-conscious, fancy hairdo

Master Bully – Muscular and intimidating, but comical

Teacher – Very authoritative, sense of power

Michael Ford

**Sponsored by Childsplay and
Rising Youth Theatre,
Tempe/Phoenix, Arizona**

My name is Michael Ford, and I'm in the seventh grade at BASIS Charter School in Chandler, Arizona. In my free time I enjoy playing video games and reading. My favorite classes include History, English, and Biology. My favorite writers are J.K. Rowling, Jeff Kinney, and Rick Riordan. Also, Dwayne Hartford at Childsplay Theater in Tempe, Arizona, had a positive impact on my writing through acting classes and playwriting workshops. I entered the competition because I loved writing and I thought it would be something fun to try. I think theatre and art can inspire change by getting the audience more involved with the characters and stories that you show them, more so than if it was simply explained to them. My best theatre experience was in a Childsplay conservatory class when we learned about the full production of a play. We assigned directors, writers, set designers, costume designers, and sound managers. We acted in each other's plays and shared them with an audience. I wrote a play called *America, More or Less*, a comedy about the founding of the United States. I really loved seeing everything come together and watching my play come to life.

Childsplay

Founded in 1977, Childsplay is a nationally and internationally respected professional theatre company whose chosen audience is children. At Childsplay we believe that young people deserve to experience challenging, thought-provoking theatre of the highest artistic quality. Our respect for children's intelligence and creativity drives us to produce new and innovative works by theatre's finest artists. Equally, our understanding of the challenges facing Arizona's classroom teachers leads us to offer arts education resources in 40 communities annually. In the past 36 years, we have educated and inspired more than four million young people and families. We have grown to serve an average annual audience of 200,000 students, teachers, and families.

Rising Youth Theatre

Our mission is to create youth driven theatre that is riveting and relevant, challenging audiences to hear new stories, start conversations and participate in their communities. We believe in the radical potential of youth; in creating art that is embedded in and reflective of our community; that everyone who wants to see or participate in theatre should have access to it; in what is possible when people from different ethnicities, genders, ages, social circumstances and cultural contexts come together; that youth deserve to see themselves, their values and their experiences reflected onstage in making great art.

Beginning of play. Nate, center stage, sorting trading cards of some sort.

FRED/FRANCINE   *(Enters in a panic.)* Nate! Nate!

NATE/NATALIE   *(Rising.)* Fred, what's wrong?

FRED   It's the Prince! He's been captured!

NATE   Captured? By who?

FRED   Bully Goblins! They took him in the night!

NATE   But everyone knows Bully Goblins can't touch a person if their self-esteem isn't low enough!

FRED   They insulted his hairdo, a sensitive point for him. They don't call him Prince Mirror Gaze for nothing!

NATE   We must save him at once! Hurry, to the S.S. Nerdprow!

Ship enters, Nate and Fred climb aboard, Prince Mirrorgaze enters, but as a narrator.

PRINCE MIRRORGAZE   And so they set sail that very day, and began their journey into the ocean. *(Nate stands at front of boat, pointing heroically.)* However, on their second day out to sea, they encountered a terrible storm. *(Nate and Fred stagger around stage while making whooshing sounds.)* But eventually, they sailed through and arrived at the Island of the Teacher!

Nate and Fred jump off ship.

NATE   At last, we are here, the Island of the Teacher! The only one who can truly solve our bullying problems!

FRED   I don't see the teacher, where is he? *(Beat.)* Wait, do you hear something?

NATE   It sounds like— *(Beat.)* The PA system!

TEACHER   *(Offstage.)* Fred and Nate, something terrible has happened! I have been lured into a trap set by the Master Bully! I am imprisoned, unable to stop him. It is taking all of my strength to give you this message. Nate, only you can free me and defeat the bullies. However, there is only one way to defeat such a powerful foe. *(Sword descends from above, spotlight directly on it.)* This is the Sword of Confidence. Confidence in yourself is the only way to defeat the Bully. *(White noise, followed by Yoda's voice.)* Good luck, young Jedi, and may the Force— *(Cuts off and returns to Teacher's voice.)* Deepest apologies, I cannot keep this up much longer. The PA system is starting to glitch out. You know... *(Getting deeper and slower.)* I think I'm going to ... stop.

NATE   The teacher captured by the Master Bully? This is worse than I thought!

FRED   Come on, Nate! Let's go!

NATE   *(Running with Sword out in front of him.)* For Pokémon!

Scene shifts to Master Bully's castle. Master Bully stands in front of Prince Mirrorgaze, who is tied to a chair.

MASTER BULLY   Muhahahahahhahahahahah! Now that I have captured you, all I have to do is wait for Nerdy Nate to come save you, and I shall finally rule the school! Muhahahahahahhhahaha!

PRINCE MIRRORGAZE   Nate isn't going to fall into any trap of yours. He's smarter than that. Just you watch!

NATE   *(Running in heroically.)* Mirrorgaze, we've come— *(Trips over shoelace and sprawls out on floor, but quickly grabs the Sword again and continues.)* We've come to rescue you!

MASTER BULLY   *(Clapping slowly and sarcastically.)* Well, very impressive. But let's see how heroic you look in my cage of taunting! *(Cage comes down, trapping Nate.)* Muhahahahhahahahaha! Oh, won't the teacher love to see how her little adventurer ended up!

Glass box is rolled on, with Teacher inside.

TEACHER   *(Facepalming.)* Oh Dear!

MASTER BULLY   Now, to lower your self-esteem bit by bit. Let's see … Where to start … Oh yes! I thought Pokémon was a baby's game! Yu-gi-oh is for losers!

NATE   You better stop that.

MASTER BULLY   Why should I … NERD?

Sneers.

NATE   Because, you don't scare me.

MASTER BULLY   What, I don't?

NATE   No! Actually, I bet you're more scared of me and of this Sword of Confidence in my hand! In fact, I'll bet—

Slashes straight through bars of cage with a loud clanging sound.

MASTER BULLY   That's—that's impossible! No one can escape when they're trapped by taunts!

NATE   They can if they have confidence!

MASTER BULLY   ENOUGH! I will finish you once and for all!

NATE   Are you challenging me to a battle? You don't even have a sword!

MASTER BULLY   Oh, but you don't need a sword for— *(Beat.)* A DANCE battle!

Multicolored lights begin flashing as Survivor's "Eye of the Tiger" plays. Nate sets down sword and begins circling Master Bully. Prince Mirrorgaze and Teacher begin cheering wildly. Nate breaks out into the disco, in which Prince Mirrorgaze and Teacher cheer. Master Bully shoves Nate and starts doing the sprinkler, followed by loud boos from the captives. Nate does the diver, resulting in more applause. Master Bully does the electric noodle, which is not well received. Nate grabs Master Bully and launches into the tango. He waits for Master Bully to spin, and grabs the sword and makes a wide cutting motion. Master Bully falls to his knees.

MASTER BULLY   Confidence ... too high ... intimidation ... useless ... ALL RIGHT! You win! But mark my words: Standing up to one bully won't stop them all. You and your people will be taunted and scared for years to come! Muhaha-hahahahahahaha!

TEACHER   I'll be the judge of that! From now on, anyone caught bulling another student shall face HARSH PUNISHMENTS!

MASTER BULLY   What kind of punishments?

TEACHER   You don't want to know. But today, I'll let you off with a warning, and a mere two weeks of helping me after school.

MASTER BULLY   Wha—? *(Teacher glares)* Yes, sir/ma'am.

Fred enters as Narrator.

FRED   And so, it all ended up all right. Prince Mirrorgaze started his own hair salon, Fred and Nate won first place in the Bakugon tournament, and the Teacher purged the school of bullies. With the help of the Master Guidance Counselor, that is.

END OF PLAY.

SCRIPT 2

Bullies Anonymous

By Chloe Rust

Characters:

Tristan – The loner with no friends who doesn't know how to communicate with people

Zack – The socially awkward cyberbully

Tony – The jock who is convinced that all the girls are in love with him

Stephanie – The passive-aggressive gossip with only two friends

Kristen – The group leader/counselor, who believes strongly in world peace, talks in metaphors, is extremely calm and kind of cheesy, very supportive and energetic

Chloe Rust

Sponsored by Oregon Children's Theatre, Portland, Oregon

Name, grade at time of contest, name and town of school:
Chloe Rust, 8th grade, Lakeridge Junior High School in Lake Oswego, Oregon.

What are your hobbies and/or favorite classes?
Hobbies: acting, singing, playing the piano.
Favorite classes: English and math.

Who are your favorite writers or other influences in your writing?
Jane Austen, Walt Whitman, Victor Hugo.

How do you think theatre (and art in general) can inspire change?
Theater conveys emotions and raises awareness in the audience.

What has been your favorite theater experience (either as an artist or audience) and why?
My favorite theater experience was seeing a staged reading of my own play and watching as my characters came to life on stage.

Oregon Children's Theatre

Located in Portland, Oregon Children's Theatre (OCT) was founded in 1988. OCT's mission is to advance growth, development, and creativity of young people through exceptional theater experiences. Our vision is to give every child in the region the opportunity to learn and thrive through the performing arts. We are proud to be the region's flagship performing arts company for young audiences, reaching more than 120,000 people every year. We are committed to both excellence and access, and we approach all of our work with respect for the intelligence and creativity of children.

Scene opens up to five chairs in a semi-circle, two of which are empty. Tristan, Tony, and Zack are sitting. Stephanie enters later. Zack glances at Tristan.

TRISTAN   *(To Zack.)* What are you looking at?

ZACK   Nothing! Um, nothing. *(Whisper.)* Geez.

TRISTAN   *(Standing up.)* What did you say?

ZACK   Nothing!

The two are standing face-to-face staring at each other. Kristen enters.

KRISTEN   *(Calmly, encouragingly.)* Hello there, you two! If you don't mind, I'd like to start this session off nonviolently. Thank you!

Zack and Tristan stare at Kristen for a few seconds before taking their seats. Stephanie enters.

STEPHANIE   *(Annoyed.)* Is this the Bullies Anonymous meeting?

TRISTAN   *(Laughs.)* What the heck are you doing here?

STEPHANIE   I'm just here hunting elephants, care to join me?

TRISTAN   Shouldn't you be at the mall with your posse?

STEPHANIE   *(Snaps picture of Tristan in the middle of him speaking, laughs.)* Nice expression.

TRISTAN   What did you do that for?

STEPHANIE   Instagram.

ZACK   *(Laughing.)* You already have twenty-four likes … twenty-five now!

KRISTEN   *(To Stephanie.)* Excuse me, but it is absolutely not okay for you to post a picture of someone on the Internet without their consent. And young man, you need to apologize for what you said. It was incredibly rude.

TRISTAN   My name is Tristan! And what about Stephanie? She just posted an embarrassing picture of me on the Internet! Nobody takes pictures of me without my permission. I prefer to live in the depths of the shadows.

TONY   (Laughing.) Shadows of other DKs.

Other bullies laugh.

KRISTEN   Hey! There are no "dirty kids" in this room. Here, we are all family and we must respect one another like brothers and sisters.

STEPHANIE   (Smirks.) Well, if you were my sister I'd run away.

KRISTEN   This is not how a family—

TRISTAN   Lady, we are not family.

KRISTEN   DO YOU WANT YOUR CERTIFICATE OF COMPLETION OR NOT?! (Takes deep breaths, in quiet tone.) Now, apologize.

ALL   (Except Kristen.) Sorry.

KRISTEN   That's better. How about we all start over on a clean slate? We'll go around the circle, tell everyone your name, then answer my first question.

TONY   Uh, we already know each other. We happen to go to the same school, in case you didn't notice.

KRISTEN   I know that you all know each other, but I don't know you. I'll start us off. My name is Kristen, and I'm a parent volunteer here at Danquail Junior High. I enjoy helping young people find peace in their lives and make changes for the better. Young man, why don't you go next? Tell us your name and why you are here.

Kristen motions towards Tony.

TONY   I'm Tony. The school counselor threatened to kick me off the basketball team if I didn't agree to come.

ZACK   (Looking down.) I'm Zack. My parents said they'd take away my computer if I didn't come.

TRISTAN   I'm Tristan. My foster parents threatened to send me to Juvey again if I didn't cooperate.

STEPHANIE   My name is Stephanie. My hairdresser sent me.

TONY   What?

STEPHANIE   It's a long story.

TRISTAN   That's the stupidest thing I've ever heard! You're here because of your hairdresser?

STEPHANIE   It's better than being sent to Juvey, stupid!

TRISTAN   Hey! I've only been there once!

KRISTEN   All right, that's enough, no pointing fingers please. How about we move on to my next question? How do you think your hormones and puberty have affected your emotions towards others?

Bullies all start talking at once, surprised and angry about the question.

STEPHANIE   Oh, please! Don't tell me you're one of those people.

TRISTAN   My hormones are fine! I don't need// your help.

ZACK   This is not worth keeping my computer.

TONY   Do we really need to talk about this—

KRISTEN   It's just that sometimes puberty can bring on a lot of emotions, but I guess that's a bit of a touchy subject. That's okay, you don't have to answer. Now I'd like to talk about why you bully others and how it makes you feel. This will help us get to the heart of your problems and bring out your inner peace.

STEPHANIE   How about no?

KRISTEN   Stephanie, I understand that this is foreign to you, but I promise you'll warm up to it. Tristan, why don't you start us off? Why do you treat others the way you do?

TRISTAN   Oh jeez, I don't know. I guess it just makes me feel good? I love the feeling of my victim's flesh below my fist. I almost think of it as a metaphor; I am the universe, and my victim is a puny star exploding into a supernover.

ZACK   Um, it's *supernova*.

TRISTAN   Only a lame geek like you would know that!

ZACK   I'm sorry, what I meant to say was —

TRISTAN   Shut up!

STEPHANIE   I think we all understand why he's been to Juvey so many times now.

TRISTAN   I told you, I've only been there once!

KRISTEN   Please, calm yourselves. That was really interesting, Tristan. So you like feeling big and strong, and it makes you feel good? Is there anything else that might make you feel equally as good without harming others?

TRISTAN   Well, I've been thinking about trying out drugs.

KRISTEN   No! God, no, that isn't nearly what I meant! Um, how about trying a punching bag? A punching bag is a great way to take out your anger quietly.

TRISTAN   You want me to take all my anger out on a stupid sand-filled bag? No way.

KRISTEN   Tristan, if you want to earn your certificate of completion, you have to agree with what I say.

TRISTAN   *(Not convinced.)* Fine.

KRISTEN   Great! Now that that's settled, let's move on to Zack.

ZACK   So, um, yeah. I'm not very good at talking to people face to face, so I talk to them using instant message or other forms of technological communication. *(Starts to rise out of his seat.)* As I talk to people, my words flow out like milk flows out of your nose when you laugh. The truth comes out like poetry on paper. *(Raises his fist.)* I can't help it … I was born to be a writer. But the marks I leave on other people are too often scars.

Pauses with his fist in the air, then returns to his seat.

TONY   That was beautiful.

ZACK   *(Surprised.)* What?

TONY   I said that was terrible!

ZACK   *(Looks down.)* Oh.

KRISTEN   Tony, why on earth would you say such a thing? I don't appreciate the way you are treating Zack. Please apologize to him.

TONY   Sorry.

KRISTEN   *(Cheerfully.)* Good! Now back to Zack, I think instead of focusing on the negatives in people you need to focus on the good in them. Try giving them compliments next time.

ZACK   Gee, I don't know. I'd rather someone tell me they hate me than lie and give me compliments then laugh behind my back.

STEPHANIE   Oh, don't worry. I'm sure people do that already.

ZACK   Hey! The difference between a new computer and your opinion is that I want a new computer!

STEPHANIE   Oh, just give up. You're not good at talking to people at all.

ZACK   At least my hairdresser doesn't control my life.

Stephanie starts to talk back; Kristen stops her.

KRISTEN   *(Slowly losing it.)* Stephanie! Zack! Please! There will be no talking back in this room. This is a bully-free zone. Now, Stephanie, tell us your story.

STEPHANIE   I don't want to, but I guess I don't really have a choice.

KRISTEN   I don't like your attitude, Stephanie.

STEPHANIE   You're not my mom.

TRISTAN   It's not like you listen to your mom, either.

KRISTEN   SHUT UP! *(Startled by her voice.)* Please. Stephanie, you don't have a choice.

STEPHANIE   Okay, fine. So, there's this girl named Amanda Fleckenheimer at my school, and she's really weird. My two friends and I kind of accidentally started some rumors about her, and it turns out my hairdresser is her mom. Normally, instead of taking this stupid class, I'd just find another hairdresser, but she's too good to lose.

KRISTEN   You're not interested in being nice to Amanda? Maybe you two could be really good friends if you were nice to her.

STEPHANIE   I don't want any other friends … I have enough.

KRISTEN   I thought you only had two.

STEPHANIE   Yeah, but that's because everyone else at my school is a loser.

Other bullies act offended.

TONY   Oh, wow, thanks.

KRISTEN   Stephanie, I want you to befriend this Amanda girl. Okay?

STEPHANIE   What if she doesn't want to be my friend? Besides, she says bad things about me, too. You don't know my life or Amanda's, so stop telling me what to do.

KRISTEN   *(Sternly.)* You will befriend Amanda. Okay?

STEPHANIE   *(Clearly not meaning it.)* Okay.

KRISTEN   *(Suddenly in a better mood.)* Great! So that just leaves Tony.

TONY   I don't bully people; everyone likes me.

KRISTEN   Are you sure about that?

TONY   Well … I did push someone's head into a locker yesterday … and I kissed my girlfriend's best friend…and…okay fine, I guess I'm sometimes mean to people.

KRISTEN   Self-admittance is the first step to recovery. The question is, why do you do what you do?

TONY   My talent is picking up chicks. So what if I have a girlfriend? That's not very fair to all the other girls that want me, is it? So I try as hard as I can to spread all my flirting with all the cute girls. But, of course, there's always competition. I'm not the only hot guy in school, but I am the toughest. So the best way to get them out of my way is to make them look like wimps, which is surprisingly easy, noting my height and extremely muscular arms.

Stephanie groans and rolls her eyes.

KRISTEN   Oh my, well I'm sure that soon your girlfriend will find out about you kissing her friend. In the meantime, apologize to everyone you've hurt.

TONY   I can't apologize to everyone! That'd make me a wimp. I think I'll just break up with my girlfriend instead.

KRISTEN   Tony, I think you know what the right thing is to do.

TRISTAN   I don't think he does.

TONY   At least I'm not in Juvey!

TRISTAN   THAT WAS ONE TIME!

TONY   How are we supposed to believe you?

TRISTAN   Oh, and you believe that Stephanie's hairdresser sent her here?

STEPHANIE   Do you think I'm proud of this? I didn't choose to be here!

ZACK   I'm scared—

KRISTEN   EVERYONE! STOP THIS RIGHT NOW! IF YOU KEEP UP WITH THIS ATTITUDE YOU WILL NEVER GET YOUR CERTIFICATE OF COMPLETION! YOU'LL BE SENT TO JUVENILE HALL, KICKED OFF THE BASEBALL TEAM, HAVE YOUR COMPUTER TAKEN AWAY, AND YOU'LL BE FORCED TO GET A NEW HAIRDRESSER. IS THAT WHAT YOU WANT?!

TONY   I play basketball, smartness.

KRISTEN   THAT'S IT! YOU ALL HAVE FINALLY PUSHED ME PAST MY LIMIT! DO YOU WANT MY HELP OR NOT? YOU ARE GOING NOWHERE IN LIFE AND THIS CLASS IS YOUR ONLY HOPE!

Kristen looks up, gets calm.

KRISTEN   When I was in seventh grade, I had glasses. They were big, fat, and nerdy. Everybody made fun of me. One day, I lost it. A girl came up to me in the hallway and whispered, "Nobody likes you, just go die already." I punched her in the stomach without even thinking, and after that it just kept going. I got rid of my glasses and changed my entire look, and soon everyone was terrified of me. The tables were turned. I felt so in control, but eventually it came back to me. When high school started, people weren't as afraid of me. One night, it became too much. I wrote a note to my parents apologizing, then got ready to leave the world, pills in my hand. No one tried to stop me; I didn't have any friends. I was just about to swallow the pills, when my mom walked in. What would've happened if she didn't stop me? I wouldn't be here. And it all started with that one girl in seventh grade. I don't want any of you to be that person that puts someone over the edge, because we die; all of us. But some sooner than others.

Kristen snaps back into reality, then runs out of the room.

TRISTAN   Whoa.

ZACK   I never really thought of it that way …

Long pause.

TRISTAN   Well, I guess that's it! Let's go —

STEPHANIE   No! I need to get my certificate of completion! I have split ends! And you need yours, too, unless you want to get sent to Juvey for the third time.

TRISTAN   Second time! And besides, I'm sure your hair would look fine without your stupid hairdresser.

STEPHANIE   *(Hesitantly.)* You think my hair looks good?

TRISTAN   *(Taken aback.)* No! I never said that! Well, I mean, it looks fine … I don't know! Just shut up!

STEPHANIE   So much for being nice.

TONY   Guys! Stephanie's right. We all need our certificates, so we have to wait for Kristen.

ZACK   I feel kind of bad for the way we treated her.

STEPHANIE   Yeah, she got pretty emotional.

TRISTAN   Oh, please. It's not like we don't act like that every night.

TONY   No … it is like we don't act like that.

STEPHANIE   Yeah … are you saying you flip out at your parents like that every single night?

TRISTAN   Foster parents. And I guess they just make me mad a lot.

STEPHANIE   How do they make you mad?

TRISTAN   It's none of your business!

STEPHANIE   You know, maybe Kristen is a little stupid, but I think she was right with saying that talking about your problems helps. My shrink says that, too.

TONY   *(Surprised.)* You see a therapist?

STEPHANIE   *(Defensive, angry.)* What makes you surprised? You know, my life isn't as perfect as everyone thinks it is. People treat me badly, too. People spread nasty rumors about me behind my back, they sneak notes in my locker; it's terrible. It's been going on since sixth grade and there's nothing I can do to stop it.

TONY   Have you talked to the school counselor?

STEPHANIE   Yeah, but she didn't do anything about it.

TONY   People say mean things about me, too. My friends make fun of me for being a grade ahead in math, and people who don't know me make fun of me because they think I'm stupid.

ZACK   You're a grade ahead in math?

TONY   I'm in your math class, idiot!

ZACK   Oh yeah … it's kind of hard for you to notice people when people don't notice you.

TRISTAN   Yeah, well, imagine having those people be the people who feed you.

STEPHANIE   I guess we all have more in common than we thought.

TONY   *(Laughs.)* Yeah. Can you imagine what our friends would say if they could see us right now?

TRISTAN   *(Shyly.)* Well, actually, you guys are the closest I've had to friends in a while.

Awkward silence, interrupted when Zack goes to hug Tristan.

TRISTAN   *(Laughing.)* Get off of me, weirdo!

Everyone laughs.

STEPHANIE   So who's in for some ice cream?

ZACK   But don't we need our certificates of completion?

TONY   We should probably give Kristen some time to cool off. We can get our certificates tomorrow.

TRISTAN   Yeah, I have a feeling the meeting tomorrow will be a lot better anyways.

TONY   *(Very serious.)* You know guys, I feel like we've all really changed today.

Pregnant pause, all bullies contemplate this idea, then laugh it off.

TRISTAN   Yeah, something like that.

All exit, lights go down.

END OF PLAY.

SCRIPT 3

Founding's Day

By Joshua Curry

Characters:

Hytern – A schoolboy from a small town. Supportive and optimistic

Jingriel – The tall, dark, somewhat shy cousin of Hytern. An outcast

Narsham – A boy from the village who bullies Jingriel

Mother – The kind mother of Hytern. Strives to raise Hytern well

Teacher – Hytern's teacher and the director of the village's Founding's Day Parade

ABOUT THE AUTHOR

Joshua Curry

Sponsored by Lexington Children's Theatre

I am Joshua Curry, an eighth grader at Sayre School, in Lexington, Kentucky. I enjoy reading and reflecting on the world around me. I believe theatre transports people to a level where they can sympathize with a character they may otherwise ignore. People listen to the messages in performances and can be moved to ignite a positive change in their world. My experience in theatre has showed this to me, and I have had the privilege to feel both the sense of invincibility that working on a production provides, as well as the profound feeling of sympathy aroused in an audience member, accompanied by the burning desire to rise and change all that is unjust in the world of the character.

I entered this competition as part of the Jr. Company program at the Lexington Children's Theatre. I wanted my writing to tell the world that change is possible — just remember to stay true to who you are and be vigilant in the pursuit of the change you want.

Lexington Children's Theatre

Founded in 1938, Lexington Children's Theatre LCT is a fully professional, non-profit organization dedicated to the intellectual and cultural enrichment of young people. We are a values based company guided by our mission statement and beliefs. Our Mission: LCT creates imaginative compelling theatre experiences for young people and families. Our Vision: We share a collective aspiration to impart, explore, foster and develop artistry at all levels and ages in every theatrical discipline and educational opportunity. We are one of the oldest continuously operating theatres for young people in the country and are proud to be the State Children's Theatre of Kentucky.

SCENE 1

Voices offstage.

TEACHER We will finish today with a passage from the Book of the Founding. Hytern, can you read that last paragraph?

HYTERN "And so Jingatoe banished Jingraele and her offspring, for Jingraele had fouled Jhonconsian blood with that of the Durghz, and had created a race unfit for life in Jhonconso. And so it shall remain, and those half-breeds, the Durgnos, shall be ever pushed to the bottom of our civilization."

TEACHER Thank you, Hytern. Now, class, you can go. Don't forget we start rehearsal for the Founding's Day parade tomorrow!

SCENE 2

HYTERN *(Enters.)* I can't wait to get home! My cousin, Jingriel, is coming to visit for the first time. His mother thinks that he can learn something in this village. I don't know what, I'm just happy to see him. *(Runs into his home.)* I'm home!

MOTHER *(Enters.)* Hytern, do you have everything ready for your cousin?

HYTERN Oh, yes, I do. Mother, isn't it fantastic? I'll finally have someone to play with.

MOTHER Well—

HYTERN Do you think he'll like my gravel collection? Do you think I could show him my favorite trees to climb? Do you think he'll like us?

MOTHER Well—

Knocking.

HYTERN He's here! *(Hytern runs to door. If need be, he could run to the other side of the stage to go to pull Jingriel on.)* Oh, I can't wait—

Jingriel enters. Hytern halts abruptly.

HYTERN (*Shocked.*) You're … You're a Durgnos … A half-breed.

JINGRIEL (*Awkwardly.*) Are you … (*Consults card.*) … Hytern?

MOTHER Yes, he is. You must be Jingriel. Welcome to our home. Come in.

HYTERN (*Still shocked.*) Yeah. Come in.

MOTHER I think you two should get to know each other. Hytern, why don't you show Jingriel to your room? I'm sure he will want to unpack.

HYTERN (*Still in a daze.*) Okay … Come on. (*He hesitantly extends his hand to Jingriel, who grasps it.*) I have this really interesting gravel collection.

They exit.

MOTHER Maybe I should have told Hytern that Jingriel was a Durgnos sooner.

She shakes her head and follows Jingriel and Hytern.

SCENE 3

Mother, Hytern, and Jingriel are eating breakfast. Hytern seems to have recovered from his previous shock.

HYTERN (*Eating a piece of bread.*) So, how do you say *bread* in Durghz?

JINGRIEL *Turshta.*

HYTERN And *table?*

JINGRIEL *Murton.*

MOTHER How about, *Hytern needs to go to the Founding's Day Parade practice. The event is tomorrow.*

JINGRIEL   *Nursht Hytern fwa rshtwi Cerv Nuntan.* What parade?

MOTHER   It is Hytern's turn to play the lead in the parade on Founding's Day.

JINGRIEL   What's Founding's Day?

MOTHER   It's the Jhonconsian New Year's. On that day, Jingatoe landed on Jhonconso and burned the ship her people arrived in, proclaiming Jhonconso its own country. You should go with Hytern to practice and see what it's about. They always do such a great job.

HYTERN   That's a great idea, come with me! And if anyone says anything about you being a Durgnos ... Well, they won't. Let's go!

He takes Jingriel's arm and runs offstage. Mother clears the table and exits.

SCENE 4

Jingriel, Hytern, Narsham, and Teacher are onstage.

TEACHER   Thank you for showing up Narsham, Hytern. You know I picked you to reenact the Founding this year because I believe you are the best. Now, Hytern, I see you have brought a guest? You realize that ... it ... is—

HYTERN   My cousin. He's my cousin.

TEACHER   Of course. *(Pause.)* Your cousin, the Durgnos, can watch. I want you all to wait a moment while I get the supplies.

Teacher exits.

NARSHAM   *(To Hytern.)* What's with the Durgnos? Has your mother finally decided to replace you with something better?

HYTERN   I already told you who he is.

NARSHAM   Yeah. Your cousin. Is that why you never talk about your aunt? You don't want people to know that she ran off with those crazy backwards savages, the Durghz?

Jingriel rises, infuriated.

HYTERN   Be quiet, Narsham.

NARSHAM   I'm just saying. You better watch out. These freaks are dangerous.

Narsham suddenly grabs Hytern by the arm and throws him to the ground. Hytern lets out a strangled cry and clutches his leg. Teacher enters, carrying five torches. She hands them to Narsham and runs to Hytern.

TEACHER   What happened?!

NARSHAM   This Durgnos just went crazy! It just grabbed Hytern and shoved him.

JINGRIEL   I didn't—

TEACHER   Silence! I shouldn't have let you stay here, with such barbarian instincts typical of a Durgnos. Because of you, we don't have a lead, and with the parade tomorrow, too.

NARSHAM   I could be the lead.

TEACHER   No, Narsham. You got to do it last year. It wouldn't be fair to all the others if you got to do it twice. Besides, I need you to push the cart to the center of town. You're the only one of my students who can do it. I truly don't know what we'll do. Perhaps we won't have a Jingatoe this year. In the meantime we should go home and think about it.

Jingriel picks up Hytern and starts going offstage.

TEACHER   On second thought, perhaps I should take you home, Hytern. I wouldn't trust you with that ... thing. Come along.

Teacher takes Hytern and exits.

NARSHAM   Nice job, Durgnos. Now, she won't let me be the lead. *(Snorts.)* You better follow Hytern, or else you'll get lost and have to slink back here like the animal you are. Good luck.

Jingriel makes a fist, but then turns and runs offstage.

SCENE 5

Hytern and Jingriel enter. Hytern is still supported by Jingriel.

JINGRIEL   Sorry about messing up your rehearsal.

HYTERN   You didn't do anything; it was all Narsham.

JINGRIEL   Maybe, but that doesn't change the fact that you're too hurt to be in the parade.

HYTERN   That is a problem. We need a lead … I know! You can be the lead.

JINGRIEL   Me?! But—you heard what your teacher said. I can't do anything; I'm a Durgnos.

HYTERN   So? Listen, you can hide in the cart, and all you have to do is act out the part when you arrive at the Town Square.

JINGRIEL   In front of the town?

HYTERN   It will only be for a few seconds!

JINGRIEL   But what if everyone recognizes me as a Durgnos? What if they hurt me? What if they all come and kick me and punch me..? Just because I'm a Durgnos.

It should seem that Jingriel is saying something that he has been thinking to himself for his whole life. He should have some trouble in voicing this thought that has plagued him always.

HYTERN   Hang on, Jingriel, listen! I am your cousin. And Durgnos or not, you're mine. And we're family. That means that we're stronger than anything between us, right? If people try anything, then they'll have to deal with me, okay? It'll be fine. You'll be fine.

JINGRIEL   *(After much thought.)* Okay, I'll do it. What do I do?

HYTERN *(Lets out a sigh of relief.)* Thank You. This is supposed to be a reenactment of the Founding, when Jingatoe burned her ship and started Jhonconso. We are really supposed to use a boat, but we just put a sail on the cart and it works. Anyway, the cart is paraded to the Town Square. Then, everyone lights a torch and lifts it up. That represents the burning of the ship, as well as the end of the old year and the start of the new. That's about it.

JINGRIEL Okay ... I'll try.

HYTERN Good luck.

Lights out.

SCENE 6

Narsham and Teacher push the cart slowly to center stage. Some appropriate music should be played during this scene. When the cart reaches center, Hytern and Mother enter. All should be carrying torches. Teacher and Narsham step away from the cart and face the audience. Jingriel slowly stands up. Teacher and Narsham gasp. Jingriel looks around and takes a deep breath. He lights his torch and raises it. Slowly, the rest of the characters do the same. Jingriel looks around and smiles.

Lights fade. Music ends.

END OF PLAY.

The Math Behind Amusement Parks

By Claire M. Edwards

Characters:

Henry – A student

Caroline – A student

Amanda – Henry's younger sister

Father – Henry's father

Claire M. Edwards

Sponsored by Honolulu Theatre for Youth, Honolulu, Hawaii

My name is Claire Edwards and at the time of the contest I was in 8th grade. I attend Le Jardin Academy in Kailua.

My hobbies include horseback riding, acting, and writing short stories. Currently my favorite subjects in school are English, Drama, and Math.

At this time I read too much to have one definitive favorite author, however, I really enjoy the works of Markus Zusak, Christopher Paolini, Eoin Colfer, and Michael Scott. None of these authors have really influenced my personal style of writing however Mr. Saint John, our high school drama teacher, really helped me through the process and taught me about playwriting.

I really entered the competition because of two reasons: (a) it sounded fun and (b) I thought that it would be a good way to expand my horizons in the realm of theatre. It has proved fi fit both criteria and I have learned a lot while doing it as well as opening my eyes to the numerous other aspects of theatre.

All art, and especially theatre, offer an escape to both the artist and the audience. It is that brief moment when an actor steps onstage and loses [herself] in the moment. And that short few hours where the audience can completely forget all their issues in the real world, leaving them irrevocably changed

forever. But it's not a change that can be seen from the surface it is a small change, almost unnoticeable. Theatre, and all art, initiates personal change on how we as humans view this world we live in.

It is so difficult to choose just one favorite theatre experience as an artist. I have not been involved in the craft for very long but there have been so many different experiences. As a part of the audience I would have to say the time I went and saw *Wicked* when it came to Hawaii. It was my first real production that I had ever seen and it was magical. As an actor my favorite experience is a tie between both mf Mr. Saint John's productions that I have been in. Both *Out of the Picture* and *Criminal Elements* were both such unique concepts and the two characters I played were as different as night and day. Both were very fun and rewarding experiences for me as an actor and as a person.

CONTINUED FROM PREVIOUS PAGE

Honolulu Theatre for Youth

Honolulu Theatre for Youth (HTY) produces professional theatre and drama education programs that make a difference in the lives of young people, families and educators in the state of Hawai'i.

HTY believes that drama education and theatre are unique, socially-based education and art forms that help their participants and audiences walk in the shoes of others, allowing them to expand their imaginations, enrich their lives and discover the infinite possibilities in the world. HTY works towards a future for Hawai'i in which people are culturally literate and imaginative, are critical thinkers and inventive problem solvers, with a respect for history and a sense of place in a complex world.

Founded in 1955, HTY is one of the oldest and most respected children's theatres in the country. HTY has served over five million people through school and family performances and drama education programs. Over 300 new plays for young audiences have been commissioned by HTY.

Lights up. Henry and Caroline are sitting at a table, some papers in front of them on the desk. They both scribble furiously on the paper in front of them. Henry crumples his up and tosses it onto the floor.

HENRY   This sucks! This project is due tomorrow and we don't have a single thing done. Nothing! Caroline. Stop drawing. We need to finish our math project.

CAROLINE   Oh come on, Henry, I already told you. We should do a presentation about how math is the foundation for some really cool things. We could talk about how math is used in roller coasters, art, court cases, and other things you wouldn't think of.

HENRY   No. That's the stupidest thing I've ever heard. And I've heard a lot of really dumb things from you.

CAROLINE   Wow. That was mean.

HENRY   At this point I don't care! We'll be lucky if we even finish this project on time. How I got so unlucky to have been partnered with you I'll never know, but if I manage to come up with anything by tomorrow I'll be happy.

Caroline gets up and unfolds one of the papers on the floor.

CAROLINE   I really think this one would work, Henry. It says, "The Math Behind Amusement Parks. By Caroline Johnson and Henry Gardner." And you asked me to be your partner.

HENRY   Stop it! You're not helping at all. Why can't you just grow up and work on something for five minutes without going off on some tangent.

CAROLINE   I can!

HENRY   No. You can't! That's the problem. You're always coming up with stupid ideas that won't work and then when I point it out, you accuse me of being mean.

CAROLINE   I know my idea for this one would work. It's simple, quick, and I've already done all the math. Would you just look!

Caroline gives Henry the paper she was working on. Henry looks at it then crumples it up and throws it away.

HENRY   No. Do I have to spell it out for you? Your idea is D-U-M-B. Your idea is dumb and we aren't doing it. I'm right, you're wrong, that's final.

CAROLINE   Henry! I worked hard on those problems. You know what, you can do this math project on your own if you're not going to listen to any of my ideas anyway.

HENRY   As much as I'd like to, it's supposed to be a group effort ...

CAROLINE   Apparently not. And with you it never is! Every time I get paired with you for a project you always pick the topic. In English we did YOUR book, in Science we did the physics of football. Even in History we did the Civil War instead of the Revolutionary War like I wanted to do. Why can't we do what I want for once? Well, you know what? I'm done with this! You can do this project all on your own.

HENRY   I can't believe you're acting so immature.

CAROLINE   I'm immature? Me? You're the one who won't use any ideas but the ones you come up with.

HENRY   Wow, Caroline. Wow. This is what I mean. You always blame everything on me.

Amanda enters.

AMANDA   Henry! Henry! Henry, guess what happened at school today? Wait, can I have a cookie, Henry? Hi, Caroline. Why are you at my house?

CAROLINE   I'm supposed to be working on the math assignment that is due tomorrow but Henry isn't cooperating.

HENRY   Don't lie, Caroline. You're the one who's being stubborn. I'm just saying that we can't use your idiotic idea for our big math project.

AMANDA   That's not nice. Henry, you need to be nicer to Ca-ro-line.

HENRY   Oh be quiet, Amanda. Why are you even here anyway?

AMANDA   I wanted a cookie. And I have good news!

HENRY   Well, Caroline and I are really busy right now so you should go away and leave us alone.

AMANDA   I don't wanna. It doesn't look like you're working to me. *(Pause.)* Why are you so sad looking, Caroline?

CAROLINE   Your brother won't listen to me … I came up with a great…and I mean great … idea for our math project, but he just shot it down. He called me stupid and immature.

AMANDA   That's mean, Henry. You should know better than that.

HENRY   You're five, Amanda. I'm twelve. You can't tell me what to do.

AMANDA   Oh, yes, I can! You two are gonna do Caroline's idea because it's better than yours. Your idea is bad and hers is good.

HENRY   What do you know? You're just a little girl.

CAROLINE   Henry! Don't talk to her like that.

HENRY   Oh be quiet, Caroline. Stay out of this.

AMANDA   Go stand in the corner and think about what you did, Henry.

HENRY   No.

Amanda puts Henry in the corner.

AMANDA   There. Now you can do your idea.

CAROLINE   Thanks, Amanda. Now. How about that cookie?

AMANDA   Well ... I guess you should ask Daddy first. I don't want him to get mad at me.

CAROLINE   Oh? Okay. I don't think I've ever met your dad. I've hung out with Henry at school but he's never invited me over.

Henry leaves the corner.

HENRY   I didn't want you to meet my dad. He's a jerk. That's why I never invite people over.

Father enters.

FATHER   Hey, Henry. Hey, baby girl.

AMANDA   Hi, Daddy! Guess what happened at school today.

FATHER   What happened?

AMANDA   You have to guess!

FATHER   *(Irritated.)* Amanda. Just tell me what happened.

AMANDA   We had to take a reading test today and Mrs. Smith told me that I read at a first grade level! I read better than everyone in my class. Even Hannah! She said that I can take the advanced class and all you have to do is drive me to school at four every day.

FATHER   Now, honey, you don't need to read at a first grade level yet. You're only in Kindergarten. Save that for next year. Besides, I can't be driving you to school every day at four; I have important things to do.

AMANDA   But it doesn't even take that long to get to school! And I don't want to wait till next year! Because if I'm reading at a first grade level now then next year I'll be reading at a second grade level and I'd have to be moved up then, too!

FATHER   I said no. Stop pushing it.

AMANDA   But, Daddy! Can't I do it? Pretty please!

FATHER   No! Amanda, you are not going.

AMANDA   But …

FATHER   It's a silly class! I'm right, you're wrong, that's final. *(Turns to Caroline.)* Wait, who are you? Henry, I told you that you aren't allowed to have people over.

CAROLINE   I'm Caroline. Henry and I are working on our math project.

FATHER   Henry, you can't invite people over without asking me first.

CAROLINE   I'm sorry, sir. Henry and I really need to finish our project. It's due tomorrow.

HENRY   Caroline …

FATHER   Excuse me, Caroline, is it? It's not my fault that you don't understand time management.

HENRY   Father. It's not Caroline's fault …

FATHER   In fact, I will go down to your school right now and have a word with your teacher about pairing my son with someone like you.

CAROLINE   *(Close to tears.)* What is that supposed to mean?

FATHER   I think you know exactly what I mean. Unless you're too stupid to figure it out.

CAROLINE   But—

FATHER   In fact, you can go do this project on your own. I will speak to your teacher and tell him what happened, so that Henry will not receive the same grade as you.

HENRY   Father, stop! *(Father looks at Henry, stunned.)* You can't speak to Caroline like that! It's not her fault that we haven't done anything. All this time we've been arguing over what topic to choose because I've been stubborn. You can't be upset at Caroline! Just because she's made a mistake or said something you don't like doesn't give you the right to tell her she's stupid.

FATHER   You and I will have words later, Henry. Have your friend call her mother to take her home.

Father exits.

AMANDA   Sound familiar, Henry?

HENRY   What—?

AMANDA   That's what you've been doing to Caroline. You and Daddy, you two are exactly the same. I've seen it since … (Thoughtful pause.) … well … a long time ago! But I didn't want to say anything because you would be mad.

HENRY   I am NOTHING like our father! He's horrible! He never listens to us! Every time that you or I want to do anything that he doesn't like he shuts us down! He tells us that our ideas are wrong and all we should do is listen to him! It drives me mad! He's rude, and mean, and neither you nor I can ever get a word in edgewise! I had to grow up with this, dealing with his mood swings and hurtful words, I don't want you to have to deal with that! It's just … It's just not right! What kind of person does that?

CAROLINE   You … you do, Henry. You do the same thing.

Silence.

HENRY   No, I don't.

AMANDA   You do too.

She exits.

HENRY   (Pause.) Caroline … we can do your idea. If you still want to.

CAROLINE   (Smiling.) All right, thanks, Henry.

HENRY   No problem. And Caroline?

CAROLINE   Yes?

HENRY   Sorry for being such a jerk earlier.

CAROLINE   It's all right.

Lights down.

END OF PLAY.

You Are Not Alone

By Riley Ellis

Characters:

Aria – A smart, caring senior in high school

Tessa – Aria's younger high school aged sister who cares about people deeply

Elmer – A smart, nerdy, and optimistic victim of bullying

Ezra – Aria's best friend. He is smart and athletic

Lilly – A pretty, popular high schooler, who thinks that she is better than everyone else

Riley Ellis

**Sponsored by University of
Texas Austin**

My name is Riley Ellis, I'm in the eighth grade at Lamar Middle School, Austin, Texas. I have been in theatre in and out of school since the first grade. Theatre is my number one hobby. My favorite classes are English, history, and dance. J.K. Rowling is the writer of my favorite book series, *Harry Potter*. I also really love J.R. Tolkien who wrote *The Lord of the Rings* and *The Hobbit*. I'd say the biggest influence on my writing would be John Greene. I find his books such as *An Abundance of Katherines* and *The Fault in Our Stars* to be incredibly touching and relatable stories. I entered the Young Playwrights for Change Competition to try writing about a realistic topic for the first time and to write a play that would hopefully find its way to someone who needed it. I wanted that someone to be able to find hope in it. I think that theatre, books, music, and visual arts are some of the best ways to carry a message. I know that, for me, I have learned more from books and movies than many other places in my life. My favorite theatre experience was playing Lucy in *The Lion, the Witch, and the Wardrobe*. The best part was at the very end of the play when I got to do a fight scene with an evil wolf.

CONTINUED FROM PREVIOUS PAGE

University of Texas Austin—Department of Theatre and Dance/ Drama Theatre for Youth and Communities

Founded in 1945 with a focus on children's theatre and creative drama, the M.F.A. in Drama & Theatre for Youth & Communities (DTYC) is nationally recognized as a leading graduate program in the field. The program continues to evolve, responding to local and global discourses related to larger concerns with drama and theatre with/ for youth and communities. The DTYC program is inherently interdisciplinary in nature, drawing on practice and scholarship from many fields such as theatre/drama with youth, education, cultural studies, performance studies, health and wellness, youth development, and visual arts. Throughout their program of study, students in DTYC participate in socially engaged and culturally responsible coursework, fieldwork, performance-making and research activities. Through drama-based pedagogy, youth-focused artistry, and rigorous scholarship, students and faculty in this area demonstrate a strong commitment to leadership, community, diversity, innovation, and social justice.

SCENE 1

A small, white room with a bed and a few other props. Aria and younger sister, Tessa, sit on the bed facing each other.

TESSA   I get it, though. I'm not sure I'm ready to leave either.

ARIA   What do you mean? You're doing so much better, Tess. I mean, look at you. You look great. You're smiling again. And you're laughing too. That's a really good sign, right?

TESSA   Well, yeah, I know. I'm just saying I think mom and dad might be right. I want to be sure that I won't try to ... you know, again.

ARIA   ... Yeah, you're right. Well, I got you something.

TESSA   *(Smiling.)* Really, what is it?

ARIA   Okay so I remember, last time I came, you said that you had been having a really bad craving for chocolate, so … *(She pulls out large box of chocolates from her bag.)* I got you these. I okayed them with the doctor and everything.

TESSA   Oh my God, Aria, thank you so much. *(She smiles widely, reaches for the chocolates, and immediately starts ripping into the box.)* I have been wanting these so badly!

ARIA   *(Smiles sadly.)* I know … I really miss you.

Starts tearing up a little bit.

TESSA   *(She looks up from the chocolates.)* Ari—

ARIA   *(Rubs her eyes.)* It's just been really different around the house without you. *(Starts crying again.)* … And I just really wish you were back.

TESSA   *(Starts to tear up a little bit too, puts down the chocolates, moves next to Aria, and puts her arms around her.)* Ari, I miss you too, and as soon as I think I'm ready, I'll come right back. But even if Mom and Dad said okay to me leaving right now, it wouldn't be the same. I'm just not ready yet.

ARIA   *(Shakes her head in understanding.)* Yeah, you're right. *(Looks up, wipes her eyes roughly.)* Just, a heads up though, I'm gonna kill those kids that did this to you.

TESSA   *(Half smiles and sighs. Rolls back onto her back and stares up at the ceiling.)* Yeah, I was thinking about that. We can't let them do what they did to me, to other kids. What if those kids didn't have a sister like you to stop them from … you know?

ARIA   *(Looks at Tessa.)* Yeah, what if?

TESSA   *(Sits up suddenly, her face lighting up.)* Hey, you make films, right?

ARIA   *(Looking confused.)* Umm hmm.

TESSA   Well, what if you made, like, a documentary, or whatever on bullying? You could do interviews and stuff. You could interview me!

ARIA   What would that do?

TESSA Well, it would show the bullies that they will not go unnoticed, and it will show their victims that they are not alone.

ARIA Well, I don't know, Tess—

TESSA Please Ari, it would help me so much to know that even a little bit of good could come out of what happened.

ARIA *(Smiles at Tess and slowly starts to shake her head yes.)* Okay, I'll do it. I'll do it for you. And I also need the film practice too. I'll use Ezra as my assistant.

TESSA Really? Thanks, Ari.

Hugs Aria.

ARIA You're welcome. *(Smiles, checks her watch, and frowns.)* Well, looks like I've got to go. It's ten minutes until your bedtime.

TESSA Uuugh, okay.

ARIA *(Stands up, hugs Tessa, walks toward the door, and pauses before she walks out.)* Tess, one more thing, why didn't you ever tell me about what they were saying to you?

TESSA I thought I could handle it.

ARIA You know that I'm always here for you, right?

TESSA *(Smiles.)* Yeah, I do.

Aria leaves. Lights fade down.

SCENE 2

First interview. After school, in front of some lockers. Ezra sits in a chair behind a camera on a tripod. Aria stands beside him, holding some papers. A boy is sitting in front of the camera.

ARIA Okay, Elmer. First question. *(Reading off of the papers.)* Have you ever been bullied before?

ELMER   Umm, yes I have.

ARIA   Can you tell us about the experience or experiences?

ELMER   Well, I've been bullied a lot, even before I can remember. When I was in middle school, the kids would make fun of my name. They would always call me Elmer Fudd, which of course makes sense. I mean who even names their kid Elmer? What good could possibly come out of that? I tried to go by my middle name, Travis. It worked for about three weeks, until a sub came in and called me Elmer again. My old name came back, and so did people calling me Elmer Fudd. I tried going by other names but people enjoyed yelling things at me like "Rabbit season!" too much. Now, people just call me Noodle, because my arms and legs look like noodles.

ARIA   Has this bullying ever affected your mental health or your performance in school?

ELMER   Well, occasionally after people say stuff to me, I just get really tired and I feel really heavy. And, sometimes I'll wake up and feel too tired to go to school.

ARIA   What would you say helps you from staying home all day every day or just really letting their comments get to you?

ELMER   Well, a lot of the times it helps to think about how this will stop. I'll become a nuclear engineer and nobody there is going to call me things. They won't care that I look like a noodle or that my name is Elmer. Probably, because they might look similar to me and they might all have really dorky names too. All I'm trying to say is that things won't always be his way for me. I mean high school and middle school just suck. Everyone knows that.

ARIA   If you had one thing to say to people who are being bullied, what would it be?

ELMER   Probably just that you don't need to change yourself. You are not the problem, the bullies are. And, it will get better. It always does.

Lights down.

SCENE 3

Another bullying filming, in a hall, Ezra is leaning against some lockers. Kids are passing by him. Aria's camera is hidden on top of the tall lockers behind him.

Elmer starts to walk by Ezra.

EZRA   Hey, Noodle!

ELMER   *(Stops, turns to Ezra, and sighs.)* Yes?

EZRA   *(Grabs Elmer's backpack. Loudly:)* Nice backpack, nerd!

People start to glance at Ezra and Elmer.

ELMER   Can I have my backpack? I have to get to class.

EZRA   What? Was that a demand?

Moves closer to Elmer.

ELMER   *(Tries to back away.)* No—

EZRA   *(Pushes Elmer. Elmer's back is now against the lockers.)* Don't talk to me like that, nerd!

People are openly stopping and staring at them now, but no one is moving forward to help.

ELMER   Please just give me my bag—

EZRA   I think the little nerd needs to be taught a lesson!

Slams his hand into the locker beside Elmer's head.

ELMER   No—

EZRA   Shut your mouth, nerd!

Pulls his fist back.

A Kid runs forward and grabs Ezra's raised arm. He yells, "Stop!" at Ezra.

EZRA *(Puts his fist down, helps Elmer off of the lockers, gives him his bag back, turns to the kid, and smiles kindly.)* Thank you. *(To the crowd around him.)* This was a planned experiment to see if anyone would stick up for someone who was being bullied. *(Takes the camera down from the lockers and points it at the bystanders.)* Every one of you, besides this guy … *(… points at Kid.)* … stood and watched as Elmer was bullied. I'll leave it up to you to figure out if that was the right thing to do or not.

Walks away with Elmer.

SCENE 4

Second interview, after school, in front of some lockers. Ezra sits in a chair behind a camera on a tripod. Aria stands beside her, holding a few pieces of paper. A pretty girl sits in front of the camera.

ARIA So Lilly, I understand that you are a reasonably popular person at this school?

LILLY Yes, I am.

ARIA Have you ever been bullied before Lilly?

LILLY No, I don't think I have.

ARIA Have you ever bullied someone before?

LILLY Sure. Who hasn't?

ARIA So, do you think bullying is okay?

LILLY Sure. I mean it's natural. It's basically human nature, to dominate over those that are lesser than you. If someone can't take it, that's their problem.

ARIA   Okay. Why do you think that those people are lesser than you?

LILLY   Well, for the same reason that I am at the top of the school, where the rest of you wish you were. I am prettier. I am smarter. And I know what people need to hear to make them give me what I want. Bullying is just the people on top's way of keeping the other people from thinking they could be us.

ARIA   Do you have any regrets?

LILLY   Well, if my bullying ever made anyone think that they are not good enough to be alive, I would regret that. That has never been my intention.

ARIA   Well, it did.

LILLY   What?

ARIA   Tessa Bennett.

LILLY   Who?

ARIA   She's a girl who you bullied. She recently … tried to commit suicide.

LILLY   Well that's bad luck. Can we get back to the questions, now?

ARIA   *(Glares at Lilly.)* Fine, if you had one thing to say to people being bullied, what would it be?

LILLY   Don't take it so hard. Just deal with it until high school ends.

Lights go down.

Back in Tessa's small white room. Tessa and Aria are sitting on Tessa's bed.

ARIA *(Finishes showing Tessa the film.)* So, what do you think?

TESSA That was perfect. It really shows what bullying is like. Thank you. *(Smiles.)* Are you gonna remove the part where you yell at Lilly?

ARIA No, I think I like it.

TESSA Well, thanks again.

ARIA You're welcome. I'm going to finish putting it together and then I'm gonna submit it to a film festival.

TESSA You'll win. That was great … I hope it shows people that they're not alone.

ARIA *(Smiles and holds Tessa's hand.)* Don't worry, it will.

Lights fade.

END OF PLAY.

Dani's Story

By Bergen Haggart

Characters:

Dani – A seventh grader who is being bullied

Emma – A mean girl who bullies Dani

Emma's Friend(s)

Leah – Dani's friend

Boy – Pushes Dani into a locker

Mr. James – School counselor

Bergen Haggart

Sponsored by Kaiser Permanente, Denver, Colorado

School:
Sixth grade, Manhattan Middle school, Boulder, CO

Hobbies and favorite classes:
Art, Piano, volleyball. Art, Language Arts

Favorite Writers:
Suzanne Collins, Yann Martel, John Green

Why did you enter the competition?
My mom asked me to share the story that I told her about my friend.

How do you think theater can inspire change?
It presents a story on an emotional level and it helps people understand the idea from the heart

What is your favorite theater experience?
I liked the props in *The Lion King*. When my own play was presented in a theater it was fun because my friends were the actors and the audience really understood what I was trying to share with them.

Kaiser Permanente

We teach. We inspire. We bring health education to life. For more than 25 years, Kaiser Permanente has brought health education to our communities through the Educational Theatre Program (ETP). Through music, comedy and drama, our live theatre programs are offered to schools and communities free of charge in each of Kaiser Permanente's eight regions. No other organization serves more children through educational theatre and nationally Kaiser Permanente employs the largest ensemble of actors. Our ethnically diverse group of professional actors also serve as skilled workshop facilitators, health educators and role models to the people they meet every day. Our programs have been presented to more than 15 million people!

SCENE 1

Emma is sitting at a lunch table, Dani walks in and Emma waves her over.

EMMA   Over here Dani Banani!

DANI   Hi M&M! What's in your lunch today? Mmmm is that a rice crispy treat?

EMMA   Yes, want half? So I asked my parents about this weekend. Your house or my house?

DANI   Your house since you've got the trampoline, the pool, AND the good cook!

EMMA   Great, remember to bring your heelies and silly bands!

The lights go out, fade to black.

SCENE 2

Dani speaks directly to the audience.

DANI   Do you think I asked for my moms to be lesbians? Well, I didn't. It's not my fault; it's not their fault either, of course. They didn't know that adopting me together would cause me to be shoved into lockers and called "faggot" every day. Those people are idiots anyway, they should know by the seventh grade that "faggot" is for boys. So what if I kinda sorta dress like a guy? I walk into the girls' locker room every day just like all the other girls do. *(Dani walks into the girl's locker room. Several girls whisper and stare. Dani ignores them.)* I know they are talking about me. I'm the joke around here. I just try to ignore them because I've found that if you pretend that you are oblivious to the meanness going on around you, and you don't react, then you are basically giving them nothing to work with, nothing to taunt and tease you about later. But sometimes, you run into the really mean ones. One that embarrasses you and makes you feel like going home and killing yourself, like Emma.

Emma walks up with a group of girls.

EMMA   Who let you in here? The boys' locker room is down the hall! *(The girls laugh and Dani ignores them.)* What's wrong, Dani? Are mommy and mommy getting a divorce? Maybe one of them will marry a man and be ALMOST normal!

Emma walks away laughing.

DANI   I don't understand. Why would one human being want to make another human being feel that way? Does it make Emma's life better to make fun of me? Does it send her to college or make her prettier? Whatever. Who needs her right? At least there is one person at school I like, Leah.

Dani walks into the main hallway and Leah walks up to her.

LEAH   How's it going, Dani?

DANI   Fine.

LEAH   Don't lie to me. What happened?

DANI   Just had a lovely conversation with Emma.

LEAH   I'm sorry.

DANI   Me too Leah, me too.

Suddenly, Dani gets shoved into the wall by a Boy, and the Boy says, "Break it up, love birds," and walks off.

LEAH   *(To the Boy.)* Leave her alone, what's the matter with you? *(Leah helps Dani up.)* People are jerks, Dani.

DANI   I don't even know him, why would it matter to him? I can't tell my moms either.

LEAH   Why?

DANI They would just make it worse.

LEAH You need to tell someone.

DANI Who?

LEAH Anyone.

DANI I'm telling you!

She takes off her sweatshirt and sits down in the hallway.

LEAH Let me see your arms.

Dani holds out her arms and shows Leah the small cuts on them.

LEAH Dani you can't keep cutting yourself. *(Beat.)* Great, here comes Emma.

Emma and friends walk up and Emma points to the cuts on Dani's arms.

EMMA Oh my God! Did you do that to yourself? I knew you were a freak but I didn't know you were that bad.

DANI It's not like I want to do this to myself, there is just no way to express my pain. It seems like the bullying will never end. I can't believe she would poke at my pain. This is her fault with all the teasing and rejection!

She stands up and gets in Emma's face.

DANI YOU did this to me.

Shouting and pointing her finger in Emma's face.

Dani pushes Emma against the wall. Emma gets up and pushes Dani back.

EMMA Back off, mister!

Mr. James runs up and pulls them apart.

MR. JAMES   Both of you in my office now. I'm calling your parents!

Emma, Dani, and Mr. James walk off stage.

SCENE 3

DANI   An hour later my moms were sitting there in the counselor's office. Emma's parents were nowhere to be seen. She looked sad and scared and I felt sorta bad for her. I asked Mr. James if we could meet just the three of us, no parents, and he agreed.

Dani, Emma, and Mr. James are sitting in chairs on stage.

MR. JAMES   Okay girls, tell me what's going on.

EMMA   She's just a freak. She dresses like a boy, she likes girls, she's just weird!

Dani looks embarrassed.

MR. JAMES   Since you are middle school girls these things happen sometimes—

EMMA   *(Interrupting.)* AND she cuts herself.

MR. JAMES   Is that true, Dani? *(Noticing Dani's embarrassment, speaks more gently.)* Let me see your arms. Look, we are going to have to talk about this more; this just got more serious.

DANI   *(Embarrassed and angry at Emma for telling Mr. James. To Emma.)* We were friends in fourth grade, what happened? Why do you hate me?

MR. JAMES   Emma, what's happened since fourth grade? Why are you behaving differently towards Dani?

DANI *(Speaks directly to audience.)* Oh great. She's just going to complain about her perfect life. She has no idea how it feels to struggle.

EMMA *(Starting to cry.)* Mom left.

The room is silent.

EMMA She and Dad fought all the time and then she just left when I was in fifth grade. Since then Dad has had all kinds of girlfriends, he's always out drinking, and he disappears for days. I haven't seen him in three days and I'm afraid he won't come back. I'm sorry I've been mean.

DANI I'm sorry that your mom left. You could have talked to me about that but you have been awful to me; I dread coming to school and I don't even like myself anymore. Why does being mean to me make you feel better?

EMMA I don't know.

MR. JAMES Emma, does being mean to Dani make you feel stronger and in control?

EMMA I don't know.

MR. JAMES Emma, you and I will meet together without Dani to address some of these other issues. Dani, I need to meet with you alone and with your parents. We need to talk about the cutting and how to deal with bullying in a more productive way than fighting back. In the meantime, can you two agree to be civil to each other at school going forward? Maybe even be friends again?

DANI   Sure. *(Speaking to the audience.)* So maybe fighting back wasn't the thing to do but keeping quiet wasn't the thing to do either. I'm still figuring it out. My moms and I are going to counseling to deal with the cutting. Emma and I have agreed to keep meeting with Mr. James. We will never be best friends again but at least we can say HI in the hallway without wanting to punch each other in the face.

EMMA   *(Whispering to Dani.)* Look Dani Banani, I still have my silly bands.

She pulls her sleeve down to reveal the silly bands on her wrist and both she and Dani look around to make sure no one else saw.

END OF PLAY.

SPONSORED BY KAISER PERMANENTE

A Little Push

By Anna Lomsadze

Characters:

Jack – A new student who is thoughtful and brave

Rachel – An energetic, very talkative student who becomes friends with Jack

Patrick – A chubby and sassy boy who is best friends with Rachel

Chris – A bully who needs to change

Ben – A person who was in the wrong place at the wrong time

Anna Lomsadze

Sponsored by Alliance Theatre, Atlanta, Georgia

My name is Anna Lomsadze. I'm in the 8th Grade at Atlanta, Inman Middle School. My favorite classes are social studies, science, and language arts. My favorite hobbies include swimming, tennis, singing with my choir, and going to the theatre. My favorite writers are Neil Gaiman, J. D. Salinger, and F. Scott Fitzgerald. I entered the competition because I wanted to combine what I believe is an issue that needs more focus (bullying) with something I love (playwriting).

I think theatre lets people see the world from different perspectives of different characters. This can inspire them to reconsider what they think about other people and issues in the world. Then, they can change to become better people. Performing, whether at camps or skits for school projects, has always been a hobby of mine. Being a completely different person for a few minutes or so lets me see the world from a totally different perspective. I also love going to the theatre. It really is a magical experience to see a show. For two hours, you are pulled into a completely different universe. How cool is that?

Alliance Theatre

Founded in 1968, the Alliance Theatre has become the leading producing theatre in the Southeast, creating the powerful experience of shared theatre for diverse people. The Alliance values excellence, pursued with integrity and creativity, and achieved through collaboration. Reaching more than 200,000 patrons annually, the Alliance delivers powerful programming that challenges adult and youth audiences to think critically and care deeply. Under the leadership of Susan V. Booth, Jennings Hertz Artistic Director, the Alliance Theatre received the Regional Theatre

Tony Award in recognition of sustained excellence in programming, education and community engagement.

The Theatre for Youth and Families component of The Alliance Theatre is under the direction of Rosemary Newcott, The Sally G. Tomlinson Artistic Director of Theatre for Youth and Families, the Alliance produces Theatre for Youth productions for elementary, middle school and family audiences in addition to the annual production of A CHRISTMAS CAROL. These productions adhere to the

Alliance mission statement and are produced with the same high standards as the adult programming.

The Alliance Education Department, under the leadership of Education Director, Christopher Moses, is highly comprehensive, engaging students from 12 months old and up. Their programs encompass The Acting School, Business Communications Skills, Theatre for the Very Young Productions, and The Institute for Educators.

SCENE 1

Jack is standing at his locker. He turns to look at audience.

JACK   It's August 7 once again. To some, that means a new year of fun and learning. To me and anyone else reasonable out there, it means the dawning of a new year of torture in this prison called school. I mean really, who in the right mind decided that school should be legal. They must have been homeschooled. Lucky them.

Turns back to locker.

RACHEL   *(Approaches Jack with a smile.)* Hey you! Are you new? *(Jack begins to reply, but she keeps on talking rapidly.)* Yeah, you probably are, because I've never seen you before. I've been here, in Santa Barbara City School since day one in kindergarten. Never missed a day of school. They better give me some sort of award for that. It takes effort coming to this school every day. You know, you're really pale. Most people in California are tan. No one can escape this state without getting at least a slight tint of brown. Some people look like actual brownies. I mean they are just brown. Anyways, welcome to this school. Oh, just some FYI, we have very lousy air conditioning here. It breaks every other day I swear, so if you see teachers dumping their heads into buckets of ice, its normal. If you have a few extra dollars, they may even let you take a piece. What's your name then?

JACK   *(Taken back, looking slightly shocked, begins stuttering.)* I uh, um, my name's uh—

RACHEL   Well get on with it! I haven't got all day! I've got things to do. Places to go. People to shoot. *(Jack gasps and Rachel begins to laugh.)* I'm just kidding. So, do you have a name or not?

JACK   *(Turns to audience with a look of desperation on his face.)* Do all people in California talk this much? By the time I get out of this conversation, I'm gonna be deaf! *(Turns back to Rachel.)* Um, my name is Jack.

RACHEL   If your last name is Sparrow then you have permission to marry me right now.

PATRICK   *(Approaches Rachel.)* Rachel!

RACHEL   *(Turns around and shouts.)* Patrick! *(Squeals and hugs him.)* How was your trip to Japan?

PATRICK   *(Sighs dramatically.)* Oh, it was terrible! All they have to eat is fish! Fish for lunch, fish for dinner, even fish for freaking breakfast! I asked them if they could fry me some pancakes, and they said they don't know what pancakes are. Talk about evolution, people stopped eating raw fish 2.5 million years ago in the freaking Stone Age! I literally spent that whole month living off of green tea Kit-Kats. *(Notices Jack and looks at him.)* Welcome to our school man. If you die, don't worry. The funeral expenses are covered. We've got a dumpster full of bodies in the back. I'm sure there will be room for one more.

RACHEL   *(Slaps Patrick on the arm while laughing.)* Come on, don't scare the little newbie.

JACK   *(Turns to audience.)* Someone help me.

PATRICK   *(Jumps suddenly.)* CPB alert! Everyone run now! To the janitor's closet!

Patrick and Rachel start running. Rachel grabs Jack's arm and drags him along. They run into a closet and peer out of the window.

JACK   What's wrong, guys? What's going on? What is CPB?

RACHEL   Shush! CPB is an initial for someone. This someone, well, you don't want to mess with him. He's going to be the end of us all.

JACK   *(Rolling his eyes.)* Well who is he then?

PATRICK   (*He takes a deep breath.*) His name is Chris P. Bacon.

JACK   (*Snorts and begins to laugh really hard.*) You, you guys are afraid of a guy named Chris P. Bacon? That's beyond hilarious.

RACHEL   No you don't understand. Here, take a look. You won't have to ask me which one he is.

Jack looks out the door window. A very large and scary looking Chris walks through the hall, stomping. Everyone around him cowers except a few followers standing behind him.

JACK   Oh my gosh.

He falls onto the door, and the door opens making him fall out right before Chris's feet.

CHRIS   Ey whatcha think you're doing? Wait. Whoa. Why are you so pale?

JACK   (*Turns head to audience while still on the floor with a confused expression on his face.*) I've been hearing that one a lot today.

Jack continues cowering.

CHRIS   Freak. Get out of my way before I kill you.

Bell rings and everyone exits into classrooms.

SCENE 2

Jack enters the stage and looks at the audience.

JACK   Well folks, it's been two months since I've gotten to this Santa Barbara City School. It's nothing like my old school in Ohio. First off, Rachel was right. The air conditioning here is awful.

In the background a Teacher with an empty bucket and the Principal enter.

TEACHER   What do you mean there's no ice left?

PRINCIPAL   I'm sorry for the inconvenience, but the ice machine is currently being repaired.

TEACHER   Are you kidding me? The job contract said I was being paid to teach kids about the effects of heat on the human body, not give them a drastic demonstration!

Teacher storms off with the Principal following him.

JACK   I heard that someone's parents were actually suing the school for child abuse, because of the heat we have to deal with. Anyways, Rachel and Patrick have become my best friends at this school. I still can't get over how weird they are, but I think them being different is sort of the best part of being friends with them.

Enter Rachel and Patrick in the background.

PATRICK   Well if Lady Gaga isn't the sassiest singer out there, then who is?

RACHEL   Beyoncé. It has to be Beyoncé.

PATRICK   *(Snorts and puts a hand on his hip.)* "Let me see your halo," says Beyoncé! No, Beyoncé. Get your lazy butt down to RadioShack and get your own dang copy!

RACHEL   Then who is the sassiest? Wait. We're so stupid. All this time we have been discussing this and we overlooked Madonna!

PATRICK   *(Gasps dramatically.)* That lady is the queen of all queens.

Rachel and Patrick exit.

JACK   That's their average conversation. I guess things are going pretty well here. Rachel says I'm going through the first phase of California tanning. She calls it the potato skin phase. The rest of the phases include doughnut, toasted bagel, milk chocolate, brownie, dark chocolate, and extra dark chocolate. I really hope it doesn't go past that. The only downside to this school is Chris. He's like a legal terrorist. People literally cower when they see him. I'm not kidding. I saw some little fourth grader get on his knees and start bowing to him. I really want to do something about him, but like the rest of the school, I'm scared. I mean have you seen the size of that kid? He could break me in half with only his pinkies!

Jack, Rachel, and Patrick are sitting together and talking, when they see Chris run past them, chasing another kid.

JACK   Guys, we can't just let him run around and treat everyone like they're nothing.

PATRICK   That's a death wish right there man. When you're gonna be lying on the ground dying, don't get mad at me.

RACHEL   What could we even do? It's not like we could just tell him to start being nice to everyone. He would just beat us up.

JACK   Well we need to make a plan!

RACHEL   You got any ideas, because I sure don't. All of them end with us being thrown into a garbage can like we're sardines.

Jack turns his head away and rubs his temples. Rachel and Patrick sigh in unison.

PATRICK   Come on guys, let's just go. We can't stop him. All we have is hope that someday a piano drops on his head.

JACK   No Patrick! We can't just let him treat us like we're nothing!

RACHEL   He's been doing that since day one man.

JACK   We just need a plan! Something that will make him listen to us. I just can't think of anything. *(He looks down for a few seconds, and Rachel and Patrick stand up to leave. Suddenly, he raises his head.)* Wait! I've got it!

RACHEL   You do? What is it? What's your plan?

JACK   I know what Chris's weakness is!

PATRICK   Well get on with it!

JACK   It's water! He can't swim! Have you noticed that during gym, if we go to the pool, he always skips class that day? He loves gym, because he can beat everyone there, but he only skips the days we go swimming! That means he can't swim!

PATRICK   Well if that's even true, which we don't know, how would we use that to help us?

JACK   We could get him into the water, and once he would be in there, he would start drowning and ask us for help! After that, he would have to apologize to us, because we saved his life!

RACHEL   You know that actually could work!

PATRICK   Well how are we gonna get him in the pool?

JACK   Um, um, oh! We can tell him that at the pool, someone left him a gift anonymously. He's so greedy, he wouldn't resist going to get it. Then at the entrance of the pool, we could put a bunch of water on the floor so that he would slip and fall into the pool!

RACHEL   The pool entrance is kind of far from the actual pool. He would fall onto the floor not into the pool. What if when he opens the door and slips, we could get Patrick to stand there so that Chris would fall onto him, and Patrick could accidently push Chris into the pool?

PATRICK   Why me? He'll kill me!

JACK   Well, we need Rachel to be the one who tells him that there is a gift basket in the pool for him, and Rachel can't be telling that to Chris and be at the pool at the same time. Then, we need someone who goes and saves him from the pool, and since I'm a better swimmer than you, sorry Patrick, you need to be the one who pushes him in.

PATRICK   Ugh, fine. This better work.

JACK   Oh it will.

SCENE 4

Patrick and Jack are standing in the pool.

JACK   *(Takes out his phone and look at his texts.)* Okay, Rachel says that she just told Chris, and that he should be coming to the pool anytime now.

PATRICK   Let's get into positions. *(He stands next to the door, and Jack stands at the side of the pool. They wait for a few minutes and Chris still hasn't come.)* Ey, Jack, is he gonna get here soon?

JACK   How should I know? Just wait.

Door opens and Ben walks in. Patrick shouts a war cry and pushes Ben into the pool. Ben comes up to the surface. Jack slaps himself in the face repeatedly.

BEN   What in the world? What was that for?

PATRICK   *(Points at Jack.)* That was all his fault!

JACK   Look man, I'm sorry. Patrick thought you were Chris. I'm really sorry. You can have my towel. It's in my locker.

BEN   *(Climbs out the pool, and exits stage annoyed.)* Shove off, loser.

JACK   *(Rolls his eyes.)* Well that was splendid.

PATRICK   Hey it's not my fault! You were the one who came up with this stupid plan anyways.

JACK   Look just— *(He cuts off and stops moving. The sound of distant footsteps appears.)* Do you hear that? That has to be Chris. Into positions, quick!

PATRICK   It better be him.

Chris enters the pool, and screams as Patrick pushes him into the pool.

CHRIS   Ahhhhhh! Mommy! Help me! Somebody! I don't wanna die!!!

Jack jumps into the pool and drags Chris onto the shore.

JACK   You okay?

Chris glares at Jack, but then suddenly begins crying onto Jack's shoulder. Jack looks up at Patrick confused. Patrick shrugs, and Jack and Patrick continue exchanging awkward glances at Chris. Rachel walks into the pool and exchanges glances with Patrick.

CHRIS   *(Begins to talk but cries while doing so.)* I hate water. That's my biggest fear. You got me Jack. Ya happy to see me like this? I bet ya are. You made all your little friends laugh at me. Great job.

JACK   I didn't mean to do that. I'm not making fun of you. I just want you to feel like we feel when you bully us.

CHRIS   *(Chris sniffles and looks up at Jack.)* You really feel like that?

JACK   Of course! That's how everyone feels when you practically terrorize us! Do you like the way you're feeling right now? Well that's the way most everyone feels with you around! You need to stop acting the way you do okay?

CHRIS   *(Starts crying again.)* I'm sorry. I'm so sorry okay? If I act nice to everyone they won't respect me anymore, because my grades suck. See this way everyone respects me.

JACK   No one respects you! They're all just really scared of you! The only way anyone will start to respect you is if you stop bullying everyone and apologize! You have to start acting differently! And if you want, I can tutor you so that your grades get better!

CHRIS   You would really do that for me?

JACK   Yeah, as long as you change the way you act.

CHRIS   You know, you're not all that bad actually. *(He stands up and grabs Jack, Rachel, and Patrick.)* Bring it in everyone.

Chris squeezes everyone together in a big hug.

SCENE 5

Jack stands facing the audience.

JACK   Chris held to his word. With some pushing from me, he went on to apologize to everyone in the school. I started tutoring him, and you know, it might take a while for him to become a straight A student, but he's improving. I guess the key thing I learned from this is you can't take out your anger on someone else, because you're not good at something, and you can't judge someone before you get to know them. Sometimes if you give someone a little push, they can gather the courage to change their ways.

END OF PLAY.

Uncouth Substitute

By Daniel Madigan

Characters:

Patrick – A quiet boy who's constantly getting bullied

Patrick's Mom – A woman who teaches her son right from wrong

Matthew – A bully

Anna – Patrick's best friend

Principal Murphy – The female school principal

Millie – The school's substitute

Daniel Madigan

Sponsored by Hartford Stage Company, Hartford, Connecticut

My name is Daniel Madigan. I'm in Grade 8 at Homeschooler Avon, Connecticut. I love making short films using my iTouch! I make all kinds of shorts Comedy, Horror and Action. My favorite class is history. Christopher Durang, Neil Simon, and Ellen DeGeneres are my writing muses.

I got the chance to interview David Hyde Pierce when he was in the Berkshires directing *The Importance of being Earnest*. After the interview, I watched the play with my parents. I was mesmerized! The play was so intriguing! After the show I decided that one day I would write a play. This year, I went on to Hartford Stage's website and I saw that Hartford Stage was having a playwriting contest! I decided to enter! I'm so glad I did! I decided my show should be about how people of all ages can be bullies. It was important to me to show kids that you shouldn't take abuse from adults who abuse their authority. I think the-atre inspires change because it's a very charismatic type of art. Theatre can be entertaining but also informational. Part of being entertained is having the brain stimulated. Some of the most famous shows deal with very serious topics. Shows like: *Macbeth*, *The Crucible*, and *Diary of Anne Frank*.

Performing as Peter Cratchit in Hartford Stage's *A Christmas Carol* was amazing. Having read the play I loved seeing how the director and cast made the show come to life.

Hartford Stage Company

Hartford Stage is the leading provider of theatre education programs in the state of Connecticut. The education department at Hartford Stage aims to provide students of all ages throughout Connecticut with innovative, quality theatrical opportunities and education programs that challenge and inspire.

Programs use theatre techniques to build community and citizenship, to promote a passion for literacy and creative expression, and to encourage life-long learning.

Hartford Stage education programs include student matinees, in-school theatre residencies, teen performance opportunities, theatre classes for students (ages 3–18) and adults, afterschool programs and professional development courses. Write On, Hartford Stage's Annual Young Playwrights' Competition for students grades 9–12, provides students with opportunities to observe professional playwrights in new play development processes. Students participate in intensive writing workshops taught by the theater's Aetna New Voices Fellow and receive readings of their own ten-minute plays. Hartford Stage was presented the 2014 Excellence in Financial Literacy Education award for its in-school residency using theatre to engage students in topics of financial literacy. The education department serves 81 towns and cities in Connecticut, and reaches over 20,000 students annually.

Hartford Stage is one of the nation's leading resident theatres, known for producing innovative revivals of classics and provocative new plays and musicals, including 68 world and American premieres. The theater's history of world premieres includes A Gentleman's Guide to Love and Murder, winner of four Tony Awards, including Best Musical and Best Direction of a Musical; Quiara Alegría Hudes' Water by the Spoonful, winner of the 2012 Pulitzer Prize for Drama;Breath & Imagination by Daniel Beaty; and Big Dance Theatre's Man in a Case with Mikhail Baryshnikov.

SCENE 1

A young boy walks down a school hallway. He is carrying many textbooks. This boy is Patrick. Patrick is eight years old. Another eight-year-old child walks out of the bathroom, he spots Patrick and walks behind him nonchalantly. This child is Matthew. Matthew starts stepping on Patrick's sneaker heels causing Patrick to become unbalanced.

PATRICK   Stop it, Matthew!

MATTHEW   Why? This is fun!

Patrick runs away from Matthew and heads outside where he waits with the other children for his parents to come as a blue car pulls up and Patrick happily jumps into his mother's car.

PATRICK'S MOM   Hey Patrick!

PATRICK   Hi Mom!

PATRICK'S MOM   So, how was school?

PATRICK   It was all right. We learned all about Christopher Columbus! However, I don't understand how Columbus was the first to discover America when there were already people there.

PATRICK'S MOM   Ha-ha! You'll learn more about Columbus later. So did you make a play date with Matthew?

PATRICK   No, I don't want him coming over.

PATRICK'S MOM   What? I thought you guys were friends.

PATRICK   We were. He keeps on being mean to me though. I think he's jealous because I made a funny joke and everyone laughed but when he made a joke no one laughed.

PATRICK'S MOM   That's rough. What do you mean he's being mean to you?

PATRICK   He keeps on stepping on my sneaker heels. I keep telling him to stop but he won't.

SCENE 2

Patrick walks down the hallway at school. Matthew sees Patrick and runs over and starts stepping on Patrick's sneaker heels. Patrick turns around, takes a deep breath and just as he's about to kick Matthew in the leg, the stage goes dark. A phone rings. Lights up on Patrick's Mom sitting on the couch at her house.

PATRICK'S MOM   Hello?

The person calling is Principal Murphy, the school principal.

PRINCIPAL MURPHY   Yes, Hi. Are you Patrick's mother?

PATRICK'S MOM   Yes I am!

PRINCIPAL MURPHY Well, today your son kicked another child in the leg.

PATRICK'S MOM Okay, what was the other child doing to make Patrick kick him?

PRINCIPAL MURPHY I-I don't know. Does it matter?

PATRICK'S MOM So, you're trying to tell me that my son kicked another child randomly? That doesn't really sound like my son.

PRINCIPAL MURPHY Uh no, no it doesn't. Perhaps this would be easier if you came to the school and talked to me face to face.

SCENE 3

Patrick and his mom are walking away from the school. Patrick's Mom turns around and looks at Patrick.

PATRICK'S MOM Patrick, hitting is never okay. I'm really disappointed in you. You should've gone to a teacher instead.

PATRICK Matthew kept pestering me even though I tried telling him to stop.

PATRICK'S MOM I understand but you should never hit someone. Okay?

PATRICK Okay, Mom. I'm sorry.

SCENE 4

Flash forward: Patrick is now in the seventh grade. He's walking down a school hallway carrying many textbooks. Matthew, the school bully walks straight up to Patrick. There's a twinkle in Matthew's eyes. Matthew slams his fist down on Patrick's books causing them to scatter all across the hall way.

PATRICK Matthew! Really?

MATTHEW   Really!

Matthew walks away with his posse standing next to him. Patrick picks up his books while Matthew walks away. Patrick sees a door to his left with a label in the middle that reads "School Principal." Patrick takes a deep breath opens the door and walks inside the room. Principal Murphy the school principal sits at her desk writing a letter. She sees Patrick.

PRINCIPAL MURPHY   Patrick! My favorite student! How may I help you?

PATRICK   Well, lately I've been having some troubles with someone. Truth be told, I'm getting bullied almost every day. If I'm not being verbally harassed, I'm being shoved into lockers or getting my books hit so they fall on the floor.

PRINCIPAL MURPHY   You did the right thing. You came to an adult instead of engaging the bully.

Beat.

PATRICK   It's strange. I know I made the right choice to come and talk to you but at the same time I feel like I made the wrong choice. Either way, at the end of the day I'm getting bullied. I feel like nothing's being done.

PRINCIPAL MURPHY   I'm confused. What do you mean by that?

PATRICK   You aren't the first teacher I've talked to about my bullying problem. Many of the teachers say that there are no bullies at our school and I feel like no one is helping.

PRINCIPAL MURPHY   Well Patrick, I promise that I'm going to fix this for you. School should be a safe environment to learn and I'm going to make sure it is.

Beat.

PRINCIPAL MURPHY   You should head to your class.

Patrick leaves.

SCENE 5

Principal Murphy is sitting with several of the other teachers in the teacher's lounge. She puts her coffee down and stands up.

PRINCIPAL MURPHY   If I could have your attention for a moment, that would be lovely. It has come to my attention that this school is developing a bullying problem. Kids are being harassed and sometimes hit. I feel that as educators we must create a safe learning environment for the children. That is why I believe we should suspend children when they hurt another classmate. I see some of you may think that we can't suspend children every time they act out but we need to show the children that there are repercussions to acting out.

SCENE 6

Anna, one of Patrick's best friends comes walking down the hallway. She sees Patrick and runs by his side.

ANNA   There's my best friend! Got a question for you! Have you seen our writing teacher?

PATRICK   Oh she's out sick. We have a substitute though.

They walk to class together. Matthew is walking on the other side of the stage. He sees Anna and Patrick and walks over to them.

MATTHEW   Move out of the way, worms.

SCENE 7

Millie enters the classroom. Millie is an old, grumpy teacher. Sadly she's the substitute.

MILLIE   Sit down. I'm your substitute. I'm taking over one of the teacher's job for two days. My name's Millie, I'm fifty-five years old, so pay your elders some respect. Get me?! Today we're going to read *Twelfth Night.*

UNCOUTH SUBSTITUTE BY DANIEL MADIGAN

ANNA   I thought we start reading Shakespeare in high school. This is the seventh grade. Shakespeare's too hard.

MILLIE   It is hard! Enough of these wizard and constipated vampire books! You worms are going to be worked to the bone!

Beat.

ANNA   Worms?

Lights slowly fade.

SCENE 8

Millie enters the teacher's lounge.

PRINCIPAL MURPHY   Hello! You must be our sub! Very nice to meet you!

MILLIE   I'm sure! I've always been told how pleasant I am. Such a shame the same can't be said for you.

Principal Murphy puts out her hand and Millie shakes it. Millie takes some hand sanitizer out of her pocket and cleans her hands. Principal Murphy walks away awkwardly toward the snack table. She starts talking to herself.

PRINCIPAL MURPHY   How uncouth could this woman be? What am I going to do?

SCENE 9

Millie's classroom. All of the children look bored or afraid of her.

MILLIE   Today, we're going to talk about choosing the right career. Now, what do some of you want to do for a living?

ANNA   I want to be an actress!

MILLIE   Good luck being poor. I tell ya, one day you're going to hit rock bottom. You know, like that Lohan chick!

Anna slumps into her seat.

MILLIE   All right, who's next? Patrick! What do you wanna be?

PATRICK   I want to be a paleontologist.

MATTHEW   Nerd alert! NERD ALERT! BEE UUU, BEE UUU!

Millie laughs.

ANNA   Hey! That's not right!

Millie looks at Anna with dagger eyes. Suddenly the bell rings. All of the children walk out of the classroom. They move as fast as they can. Anna walks straight into the principal's office.

SCENE 10

PRINCIPAL MURPHY   Anna! How may I help you?

ANNA   Well, our substitute is bullying people!

PRINCIPAL MURPHY   I understand. Believe me, I have noticed such actions. I do have a plan though.

ANNA   What is it?

Lights dim.

SCENE 11

School assembly. The entire school faculty and children walk to their seats.

PRINCIPAL MURPHY   Now, I have been seeing a serious bullying problem going on in this school. Kids are being pushed into lockers and this is unacceptable!

PATRICK   *(Stands up from his seat.)* I'm sorry. I don't mean to interrupt but I have something to say. Bullying has been a huge problem in this school and many schools all around the country. If you're getting bullied and no one listens, don't give up until someone hears you. The best way to stop bullying is to have confidence in yourself and it helps if you have a good comeback.

The whole assembly including Matthew, stand up and cheer! However, one person is not amused ...

MILLIE   Oh give me a break. *(Everyone gasps at her audacity.)* Spare me, but I cannot stand all this ridiculous "rise above it all" hogwash!

PRINCIPAL MURPHY   Kids, let me remind you that anyone can be a bully even an adult.

All of the kids semi-laugh at this, they're more afraid of what Millie's response will be.

MILLIE   I don't have to take this. Come on son, we're leaving this place. We're above this.

MATTHEW   *(Stands up from his seat.)* No, Mom.

MILLIE   Matthew. Come on!

MATTHEW   No, Mom. These people are nice. I'm taking the anger I have with you out on some guys here and ... that's not right.

Millie screams in anger and runs off stage! The kids stand up and cheer! Principal Murphy hugs Matthew. Matthew walks over to Patrick.

MATTHEW   I'm sorry for fighting with you. I really am.

PATRICK   The only fight you can't lose is the one you don't have. Thanks for apologizing though.

Matthew and Patrick walk side by side to class together.

END OF PLAY.

The New Girl

By Eugenia Montsaroff

Characters:

Douglass – A 14-year-old boy who actually rather dislikes his position as class bully, but can't seem to find a way out of that role, and definitely has some stuff going on at home.

Samantha – A 13-year-old girl who recently moved to the school from Vancouver. She has a past there, about which she does not share easily, and understands Douglass a lot more than he thinks. A possessor of far too many descriptions to accurately put here.

Eugenia Montsaroff

Sponsored by Seattle Children's Theatre

My name is Eugenia Montsaroff, and I'm in Seventh Grade at Washington Middle School in Seattle, Washington. My favorite hobbies are writing poetry, plays, and YA fantasy/sci-fi, as well as reading, acting, drawing, and playing the Clarinet. My favorite subjects are Language Arts and Math. My favorite writers are J.K. Rowling, Shakespeare, Terry Pratchett, Nathaniel Hawthorne, and Christopher Paolini. Language Arts teacher Ms. Hill is also a huge influence on her writing, as are the many lovely people on the internet who take the time to review her work. I entered the competition because I know from firsthand experience that bullying is a huge issue, and anything that I could do to bring awareness to it and make people think about it is great. I also was prompted by my Language Arts teacher to enter the contest. I think theater is far more personal than many other art forms, and because of the intimacy between artists and audience it conveys ideas exceptionally powerfully and therefore can inspire change in the world. My favorite theater experience was acting and producing Seattle Shakespeare Company's teen version of *The Tempest* by Shakespeare. The cast were all great to work with, and playing the role of Antonio is an exceptionally fun thing to do.

Seattle Children's Theatre

Seattle Children's Theatre (SCT) is one of the most prominent theatres for young audiences and among the top 20 regional theatres in the country. Our programs empower young people to make new discoveries about themselves and the world around them while building a lifelong interest in the arts. The mission of Seattle Children's Theatre is to provide children of all ages access to professional theatre, with a focus on new works, and theatre education.

Founded in 1975, SCT first produced plays in the Poncho Theatre, at Seattle's Woodland Park Zoo. SCT started as a program of the Seattle Department of Parks and Recreation, with initial funding from the City of Seattle and PONCHO (Patrons of Northwest Civic, Cultural and Charitable Organizations). Some of the earliest supporters of the organization were teachers and graduate students from the University of Washington's Masters Program in Theatre for Youth (one of the few of its kind at the time).

Since its inception, Seattle Children's Theatre has strived to provide innovative artistic programming and professional theatre for the young people and families of the Puget Sound region. SCT moved into the 482-seat Charlotte Martin Theatre in 1993, the 275-seat Eve Alvord Theatre in 1995, and completed the Allen Family Technical Pavilion, which consists of the paint, costume, prop, and scene shops as well as rehearsal and classroom spaces, in 2000. This state-of-the-art facility was the first self-contained theatre complex built for young audiences in the nation, and has since been used as a model for other theatres.

By the end of its 2013–14 Season, SCT will have produced over 235 plays, 113 of which were world premieres and entertained, inspired and educated over 4 million children.

SCENE 1

SAMANTHA *(Enters the class and goes to her desk and sits.)* Hey! I don't think that we were introduced since I came from Vancouver. What's your name? I'm Samantha, though mostly everyone calls me Sammy.

Douglass grunts.

SAMANTHA That's a beautiful drawing.

DOUGLASS Look, I try to make it my policy not to beat up new kids on their first week, but you're really pushing it. I thought I already made it clear not to talk to me.

SAMANTHA *(Laughs.)* I think this has been the earliest I've ever received a threat in a conversation. Usually people at least attempt to be civil at first, although I must say your honesty is kind of refreshing.

She begins working on her paper.

DOUGLASS   *(Mumbles.)* Doug.

SAMANTHA   Hmm?

DOUGLASS   *(Louder.)* I said Doug. My name is Doug.

SAMANTHA   *(Looking up from paper.)* That's a nice name.

DOUGLASS   I don't care what you think about my name. Or my art.

SAMANTHA   I never said you did, or had to.

DOUGLASS   And if you tell anyone I draw, I'll, I'll …

SAMANTHA   I wasn't planning on telling anyone. You don't have to worry.

DOUGLASS   I was just … just making it clear.

SAMANTHA   Sure thing.

Scene fades out.

SCENE 2

In a hallway. Douglass is at his locker. Samantha walks up behind him.

SAMANTHA   Hey Doug.

DOUGLASS   *(Growls.)* Do you even—?

SAMANTHA   Are you busy this afternoon?

DOUGLASS   … What? Why?

SAMANTHA   Can you be in the library after school at 2:30?

DOUGLASS   Libraries are for sissies.

SAMANTHA   Then call me a sissy. I need to do some stuff in the library, and I was wondering if you'd show me the ropes. School libraries can be really different from one another, and I don't want to mess anything up.

DOUGLASS   Bug off.

SAMANTHA   I was just wondering. See you there!

DOUGLASS   I said I wouldn't … ugh.

Exeunt.

SCENE 3

Samantha is reading in the library. Enter Douglass.

SAMANTHA   Hi Doug! I was beginning to wonder if you'd show up.

DOUGLASS   I'm not here to help you. I already said I wouldn't come.

SAMANTHA   That's fine. Is this the historical fiction section, or is it down there?

DOUGLASS   I already said I won't—fine. It's over there, next to the door.

SAMANTHA   Thanks.

DOUGLASS   Aren't you going to get a book?

SAMANTHA   Nope. I was just curious.

DOUGLASS   Curiosity made Doug beat up the cat.

SAMANTHA   The curious cat actually had a reason for asking. She wants to read the book *Johnny Tremain* when she's done with her current book, and wants to know where to get it.

DOUGLASS   You have no idea how easy I've gone on you kid. I swear I—

SAMANTHA   When was the last time you hit someone?

DOUGLASS   What?

SAMANTHA   You keep threatening me, but you never hit me. I also haven't seen you beat up anyone else. You don't have to answer, I was just—

DOUGLASS   *(Hits Samantha.)* —Curious. That seems to be a theme with you.

SAMANTHA   *(Rubbing the area where she has just been punched.)* It does happen to be one of my many weaknesses. That was a good hit, though I can't say that I would willingly accept another one. Try to follow through with your body next time more, but overall well done.

DOUGLASS   What? I just hit you! And you're—ugh. I give up.

SAMANTHA   All I did was compliment you and give some constructive critiques. Why are you so angry?

DOUGLASS   If you hit me and I didn't react angrily, how would you feel?

SAMANTHA   I'd be happy that you didn't retaliate, because that can lead to all sorts of complications.

DOUGLASS   You would do that, wouldn't you?

SAMANTHA   Yes, I would. Now if you don't mind, this is a really good book I'm reading and I'd like to get back to it.

She resumes reading.

DOUGLASS   What is it you want?

SAMANTHA   Come again?

DOUGLASS   You have to want something, otherwise you wouldn't have invited me here.

SAMANTHA   *(She puts down the book.)* I don't have any reason to ask you here other than the ones already given.

DOUGLASS   So you don't really have any questions for me?

SAMANTHA   Well, I do but I didn't intend to pose them. Now that you ask, though … Why do you hit people?

DOUGLASS   It's … easier.

SAMANTHA   Than what?

DOUGLASS   Just … easier.

SAMANTHA   That didn't answer my question whatsoever.

DOUGLASS   You and your … curiosity. Ugh. I don't have to answer anything.

SAMANTHA   No you don't. I just found that a friend can really help.

DOUGLASS   Help what?

SAMANTHA   Everything.

DOUGLASS   No.

SAMANTHA   *(Resumes reading.)* Suit yourself.

DOUGLASS   Wait. *(He begins to cry.)* Everything is … messed up—and don't you dare be curious about how. I just don't want to end up like …

SAMANTHA   *(She sidles over and puts an arm around his shoulder.)* Shhh …

DOUGLASS   *(After a while he stops crying.)* Now go away.

SAMANTHA   Heck no. Come on, let me grab you a tissue.

She rises and grabs Douglass a tissue box.

DOUGLASS   Are you going to tell the whole school now?

SAMANTHA   Not unless you want me to.

DOUGLASS   Sammy ... thanks.

SAMANTHA   For what?

DOUGLASS   I've forgotten what a relief it is to cry, even if it was in front of a...sissy. I know it doesn't fix anything, but, I mean ... It's like drawing ... and I just ...

SAMANTHA   I know exactly what you mean. Come on. I think the ice cream parlor I saw on my way to school is open, and if there is one item that can solve all problems it is an ice cream cone.

DOUGLASS   *(With a weak smile.)* If you insist.

END OF PLAY.

A Tale of Two Bullies

By Sophie Nicholson

Characters:

Josie – The spunky new girl at school

Sarah – A heartless and popular seventh grader

Erica – A seventh grade girl who just wants to be cool and popular, and will do anything for it

Kendall – Erica's seventh grade tag-along friend who gets pulled into the bullying mess, and can be shy at times

Mr. Doccnour (pronounced doc-nor) – The girls' quirky and young (mid to late 20s in age) seventh grade teacher, who has a feeling that things aren't right with the girl

ABOUT THE AUTHOR

Sophie Nicholson

**Sponsored by DreamWrights
Youth & Family Theatre,
York, Pennsylvania**

School:
Grade 6, York Suburban Middle
School in York, PA

Hobbies:
Dance, swimming, reading,
acting/performing

Influences:
Jennifer Nielson, J.K. Rowling

Art is something very popular that influences the things we do, and life in general. With technology native kids today, things like performing have a great influence on kids. With television and modern technology I think that art is hinted at in everyday life and that causes kids to personally change subliminally for the better.

I entered the contest because I thought it would be fun, and I would learn new things, and I might just win.

DreamWrights Youth & Family Theatre

DreamWrights Youth and Family Theatre offers an interactive theatre experience for the entire family. From camps and classes to full-scale productions of timeless tales and iconic stories, children and adults of all ages and skill levels will enjoy a hands-on theatre experience. Whether your passion is being center stage, behind the scenes, or in the audience, DreamWrights offers opportunities to explore all aspects of theatre from acting and designing to crewing and stage managing.

A non-profit organization founded in 1997, DreamWrights was created by a group of families who believed that participation in a quality theatre education program would have a profound and valuable impact on their children. While the organization continues to grow and offer new interactive and educational experiences, this common vision has never changed.

SCENE 1

Our show begins in a seventh grade classroom, after the bell has rung. Most of the students have left because they have another class to attend. Mr. Doccnour sits at his desk, while keeping a close eye on the girls. Sarah, Erica, and Kendall are whispering about the new student, while they "read" their books. As our scene starts, Mr. Doccnour gets a call from the office to come and get the new student, Josie.

MR. DOCCNOUR   Now, I have to go and retrieve the new student. Kendall, you're in charge. Did I cover everything? Kendall is in charge ... perfect! They're all ready! Now let's see if— *(Checking his list.)* Miss Josie is. *(He walks to the door and Josie is standing patiently in front of it.)* AH! Are you—?

JOSIE   Josie Kembersoft, your new student? Twelve years old, going on thirteen in February, lives at 1589 Sunset drive, and is standing at your door currently? Yes, I am. Oh, and by the way, nice tie!

SARAH   *(Whispering.)* Kembersoft? What sort of a last name is that?

ERICA   *(Continuing the trend of whispering.)* The weirdest one I ever heard! I'll bet she's weird! Did you see how she talked to Mr. Doc? *(Getting Kendall's attention by nudging her, because she had been drifting off.)* Right Kendy?

KENDALL   *(Unsure of herself.)* Sure, I guess. *(Whispering very quietly, because she is slightly scared they will get mad at her.)* We shouldn't judge her. That's really not nice to assume that she's weird. Maybe she's the nicest girl ever.

SARAH   *(Firmly and upset.)* I'm sorry Kendy, but were you saying something?

KENDALL   *(Softly because she is scared.)* No.

MR. DOCCNOUR   Josie, why don't you sit next to Kendall and Sarah.

He guides Josie in their direction.

SARAH   Remember girls, cool and confident. *(To herself.)* It's the best way to get people to obey you. Because of that, everyone wants to be me, or like me. I like it that way. I practically own the school! Every kid up to ninth grade is afraid of me! It's kind of an exaggeration ... No! It is the most true thing I have ever heard! I know if we act cool, and shoot her down, she will never have a chance to take my place.

She laughs her evil laugh.

KENDALL   *(Obviously defying what Sarah wants her to do.)* Hi Josie! I'm Kendall! Or, my friends call me Kendy! I really don't care what you call me! Whatever feels comfortable and works for you!

SARAH   *(Through clenched teeth.)* Uh Kendy, remember cool and confident?

ERICA   *(At a medium volume, just to Kendall and Sarah.)* This is how the pros do it! *(Returning to normal volume.)* Hi, uh Josie is it? *(Josie nods.)* I'm Erica. Nice last name! It's dorky, but I guess it's kind of cool?

She smiles slyly.

SARAH   Name's Sarah. Sure dorky, but definitely NOT cool!

KENDALL   *(Shyly to her friends.)* Be nice! *(To Josie.)* I like it! It's very pretty!

She smiles at Josie so only she can see.

JOSIE   *(Smiling back at only Kendall.)* Thanks! No one's ever told me that!

SARAH   *(To herself, very quietly.)* There's an obvious reason for that! *(Kendall "kicks" her.)* Ow!

MR. DOCCNOUR   Okay class, I am sad to say that homeroom is done for today. I wish you luck, in your studies today and as always, have a grrrrr-eat day.

SCENE 2

By the lockers after class Sarah, Erica, and Kendall are leaning against the lockers. Sarah and Erica are whispering to each other while Kendall is looking up as if she is day dreaming. The scene begins as Josie walks by with a small smile on her face.

SARAH   Hey look girls, it's Josie the Joke! What are you up to? *(In a babyish voice.)* Having fun in loser town? Population one? *(Josie walks faster.)* Scared? I could tell you were just a joke. Run home to mommy! *(Firmly.)* You better run!

As Josie reaches them Erica trips her.

ERICA   *(Sarcastically.)* Oops! Sorry!

Sarah laughs.

SCENE 3

MR. DOCCNOUR *(Sitting at his desk, typing, and reading his letter to Josie's parents aloud to himself.)* All right, here it goes! Dear Mister and Missus Kembersoft, it has come to my attention—no that doesn't sound right! I am your daughter Josie's homeroom and math teacher, and I am worried about her for MANY reasons. First, she hasn't been turning in her assignments on time. I believe this is because of reason number two. Which is, I have noticed that Josie is getting picked on, mainly by two students. I have noticed before she wasn't affected by the bullying, but now, she seems more sad and lonely after it happens. You should—no, might want to—no! I shouldn't tell her parents about it. I don't want to interrupt their life. But maybe—no. I'll just keep an extra keen eye on those girls, and hope and pray that it doesn't get worse.

SCENE 4

Outside of Mr. Doccnour's Classroom, Kendall approaches Erica who is leaning on the lockers casually.

KENDALL Eri— *(Pronounced "airy")* why do you and Sar insist to be mean to Josie?

ERICA Because, it's cool to be mean!

KENDALL *(Getting frustrated.)* Who ever told you that?

ERICA No one really. Sarah's mean and cool so I just assumed it was.

KENDALL It's not cool to be mean. You know, the truth is, you sometimes make assumptions that aren't true, and can really hurt people.

ERICA Since when did I ever do that?

KENDALL You've done it since second grade. Remember Rodney?

ERICA You mean Runaway Rodney? He got so scared of us, he moved! I don't care. He's gone, and that's good enough for me. Back to the cool subject. Don't you even want to be cool?

KENDALL Of course but I—

ERICA *(Cutting her off.)* Exactly! So if you just do what Sar wants—

KENDALL   *(As if she is about to scream.)* WHEN DID Sarah COME INTO THE PICTURE! *(She pauses.)* Forget it. If being cool means being mean I'm done.

ERICA   *(Kendall is now her main problem/target for bullying.)* Oh and forget about sitting at your old table. And by the way, I'm ER-I-CA. Forget about calling me "Eri"!

Kendall turns to leave.

KENDALL   *(Even more disgusted.)* This is just crazy. You don't rule the world! I'm out of here!

She exits.

SCENE 5

Our scene opens by the lockers the next day. Sarah and Erica are picking on Josie with Kendall keeping a close eye on them.

SARAH   *(As if she is complimenting her.)* Josie, I don't like your shoes! They're SO UGLY!

She grins.

ERICA   I know they're even uglier than Kendall's!

JOSIE   Why don't you like my shoes? What's wrong with them?

SARAH   *(Counting on her fingers.)* They're plain, drab, ugly, bland, out of season, huge—

KENDALL   *(Outraged and furious.)* STOP IT! You're making her cry! *(Josie sobs.)* It's not cool to be mean! Josie, I heard Mr. Doccnour wants to see you. Let's go.

They go to Mr. Doccnour.

MR. DOCCNOUR   Hi girls! Is everything all right? *(He witnessed the event so he knows what has been going on.)* Any problems with a certain two girls, whose names begin with—

KENDALL   *(Interrupting him.)* Yes, those girls have been bullying Josie since she came to Morris Junior High ... *(Shyly.)* ... And I have been avoiding telling you until now. And you know what they say, the person who stands by is as guilty as the bullies. *(Louder.)* I'm really sorry Josie. Can you forgive me?

JOSIE   Why shouldn't I? You stood up for me. Your, sort of, bullying was the past, and this is the beginning of the future. I forgive you.

MR. DOCCNOUR   Josie, is this true?

JOSIE   Sadly, it is.

MR. DOCCNOUR   And you witnessed it, Kendall?

Kendall nods.

MR. DOCCNOUR   *(To himself.)* I told you, Doccnour! I told you!

MR. DOCCNOUR   Sorry, I thought you were in a pickle and almost e-mailed your parents about it. Sorry about that! *(Josie flaps her hand as if to push the fault behind her while smiling as if to say, "Ah, it's okay Mr. D.")* Let's stop this shall we? *(Josie and Kendall smile.)* Erica, Sarah! You have some explaining to do!

SARAH   What? We didn't do anything!

MR. DOCCNOUR   I didn't even tell you what you did and I have yet to explain my reasoning. How do you know you didn't do anything? What if I asked you if you breathed today, huh? *(Tapping into his "inner teacher.")* What would you have to back you up? Remember, evidence is key! If you had waited and heard what the question was, you would have made a better argument. Now next time you answer a question before hearing it you have to consider the past and —

KENDALL   Uh, Mr. D.?

MR. DOCCNOUR   Yes, Kendall?

KENDALL   Remember why you are talking to them?

MR. DOCCNOUR   Oh, yes! *(He gets serious again.)* Sarah and Erica. Kendall and I have noticed that you two have been emotionally hurting Josie —

Kendall mumbles "Ah hem!" to signal that the girls have been emotionally hurting her, and apparently physically too.

A TALE OF TWO BULLIES BY SOPHIE NICHOLSON

SARAH   We didn't do ANYTHING! We were only kidding!

KENDALL   Sarah, it's no use hiding your secret. I heard you plotting to be unkind to Josie the day she arrived. I know you want to be popular and "rule the school" but the best way to get people to like you is to be nice to them, not to conquer them by being mean!

SARAH   How were we supposed to know? We're not geniuses! We just tried what we thought would work, right Erica? *(Now talking like her problem really has hurt her heart.)* We just want to fit in!

ERICA   Actually, Kendall tried to tell me that we were doing the wrong thing. Kendall, I'm really sorry about that. Can you, and you, Josie, forgive me?

KENDALL   Of course but, you still did the wrong thing. I wish you had seen the wrong in your ways before. I tried to warn you, and you listened but you didn't hear the truth until now.

Kendall embraces with Erica.

JOSIE   I always knew you had good in you, Erica!

She joins the embracing.

SARAH   *(Sarcastically.)* Whoop-de-doo! A happy ending! Yaaaaay!

Erica nods her head to say "Come on! Say you're sorry!"

SARAH   *(Sarcastically, and forcing it out as though it is hard to say.)* I'm sorry, I guess.

MR. DOCCNOUR   Well, I am very happy all of you made up. Sarah and Erica, you will have to face the wrath of Principal Markks. Normally, Kendall, a teacher might punish you too, since you didn't do anything to stop it when it started. But, you told me about it today, so I have no choice to— *(He pauses dramatically.)* Let you off the hook.

SARAH   Why do we still get punished? Like I said, we were only kidding!

MR. DOCCNOUR   Tell it to the judge, Sarah, tell it to the judge.

END OF PLAY.

Combo Pizza

By Darci Ramirez

Characters:

Kyle – Male, 17 years old. Has a disability that makes him socially and mentally challenged. He acts like he is no older than 10 years old, and has the reading level of a third grader. His parents are divorced, he lives with his mom, but likes being secluded at his dad's. He has a younger sister, Josephine.

Josephine – Female, 15 years old. Mentally gifted. Socially awkward at times, but not necessarily challenged. Parents are divorced, she lives half and half with her mom and dad. Not very close with Kyle, but still very protective. She is trying to make Alyssa, Ryan, and Colton into more understanding people.

Alyssa – Female, 15 years old. Not very open minded, but respects Josephine's opinions. Not very nice, but more considerate than Ryan.

Jamie – Female, 10 years old. Very much like her brother in some aspects, but still very impressionable. Not really popular at her school.

Ryan – Male, 15 years old. Alyssa's friend and is very openly rude. He has dyslexia and is very embarrassed and angry about that. He takes out his anger by mocking people.

Colton – Male, 15 years old. Very wishy-washy with his opinions, likes to agree with the group as a whole. Has a little sister, Jamie.

ABOUT THE AUTHOR

Darci Josephine Ramirez

Sponsored by Noorda Theatre Center for Children and Youth, Orem, Utah

Seventh grade, American Fork Junior High in American Fork, Utah

I love acting and the arts. I also love history, reading, science, and any sort of geekery. Musical theatre is one of my favorite activities, along with playwriting. Anything to do the arts and theatre I can't get enough of.

As far as playwrights go, I will always have a soft spot for Shakespeare, (I mean, come on! That's some deep stuff right there) but anyone who is brave enough to put out a play is inspiring in my book. My family members inspire and help me so much it isn't even funny, each in their own way. They are amazing and thought provoking and all around cool.

I wanted, and still want, to change the world for the better. So why not combine my passion for the arts in a way that's more than just entertainment for me and others?

It touches hearts in a way no one can really explain or comprehend. It can be as vague or exact as it needs to be, and it will still send a message. People choose to let it into their hearts and minds, and it can alter our being.

I had the opportunity once to be in a production where my character that I was developing was actually a real person in the 1800s, and I felt like I was carrying on her legacy. I influenced her and made them who they were in the show. It was a sort of symbiotic relationship where we both grew. Being an audience member is also touching and somewhat noble, every show is a new, awesome experience.

....

Noorda Theatre Center for Children and Youth

Founded in 2009, The Noorda Theatre Center for Children and Youth is part of the Department of Theatrical Arts at Utah Valley University. The Noorda Center produces two annual touring shows, provides outreach for the department's mainstage productions, provides production support for mainstage plays for young audiences, coordinates an associate degree, and operates a summer theatre camp for more than 200 young people.

The Noorda Center at UVU was created with the generous support of Tye Noorda, who wanted to ensure that all young people in the community have access to theatre and speech experiences that build their self-confidence and improve their communication abilities. The Center provides free or reduced tuition to more than a quarter of its summer camp students. It also offers touring productions for little or no cost to underserved audiences in rural communities, low income schools, and schools with large numbers of English language learners.

The Noorda Center is committed to the development and performance of new plays for young audiences. In 2015, it will present the first production of Suzan Zeder's *The Milk Dragon* after a two-year development process with the playwright. Wendy Gourley, the Center's Playwright-in-Residence, has written new works for mainstage, touring, and youth productions at UVU. The Noorda Center has also developed new work by Sandra Fenichel Asher.

Maria Escamilla was the "matchmaker" who introduced Tye Noorda to Katherine Farmer, who taught in the department of theatre and served as the Center's Founding Artistic Director. The Noorda Center is now led by Dr. John Newman, a professor in the UVU theatre department, with the assistance of Outreach Coordinator Eileen Nagle, who facilitated the 2014 Utah Young Playwrights for Change program.

AUTHOR'S NOTE

I would like to thank Prof. Bryan Waite of Utah Valley University for his insight on differences and his quote, "People aren't weird; people are different. And different is good."

SCENE 1

In a school commons area, sounds of lots of teenagers talking. One girl at a table alone, Josephine, reading. Colton, Ryan, and Alyssa go to a nearby table and start talking.

ALYSSA I KNOW!! What a loudmouthed teacher's pet! It's like she can't shut up for two seconds to breathe! She has to store extra air in her big head, 'cuz she talks so much!

RYAN   She must have gotten all of the brains in her family, 'cuz her brother sure as HECK doesn't have any! They have to send him to a dumb kid's – I mean "special kid's" school.

After a round of laughter, Josephine stands up so quickly that she knocks down her chair. She ignores it and goes over to the table with the other teens with a fake smile.

JOSEPHINE   Hey, guys! What ya talking about?

COLTON   *(He jumps at Josephine's sudden appearance. Very quietly.)* Oh, nothing.

RYAN   The … basketball game last night. Did you see Adam Lancer? He tripped right after he got the ball and cost the team the game. What a freaking retard …

JOSEPHINE   Sorry, a what?

RYAN   RE-TARD, kiss-up. Your brother's kind of retarded. Not like you and your special class, kiss-up, but like he's got to be stopped from eating any more glue …

Ryan laughs. Alyssa chokes down a laugh and Colton pretends to giggle.

ALYSSA   Come on, her brother can READ can't he? Oh my gosh, Jo, don't take it so personally, he didn't mean it, he was just joking. Dang, can you spell sensitive … ?

A bell rings and Ryan and Alyssa leave. Colton and Josephine are packing up their backpacks.

JOSEPHINE   What was that, Colton? Didn't you hear them? How could you want to hang around them?

COLTON   They were just joking around, it didn't do any harm, just words.

JOSEPHINE   They were making fun of my brother! You've met him, you liked talking to him!

COLTON   It was just a joke. Your brother wouldn't mind.

JOSEPHINE   Because he loves everyone. He can't think of them in a bad way! You guys were picking on one of the kindest people on Earth. Yeah, real funny.

COLTON   I'm sorry, but I don't understand why you're so ticked about this. It's not like I was saying anything. And Ryan wouldn't say that to his face.

JOSEPHINE   What's the difference? You just stood by and took it. And if Ryan can say that so easily here, why not to Kyle's face? I just really hope that you're happy with yourself.

Josephine storms off, Colton walks in the opposite direction.

SCENE 2

Kyle is onstage, kneeling like he is in front of a TV and muttering to himself.

KYLE   The Steelers are gonna beat them…four more wins and they make it to the semifinals … *(Yelling.)* NO! That's a foul! Holding, Fifteen yard penalty!!!

Josephine walks in covering her ears, but smiling.

JOSEPHINE   Hey, Kyle! How's the team doing?

KYLE   This stupid ref is blind! He can't see any-anything in front of him!

JOSEPHINE   He never can … *(Beat.)* So what's going on with you? I'm staying with Dad tonight.

Kyle looks dejected and uncomfortable.

KYLE   Oh …

JOSEPHINE   It's okay, I won't invade your cave.

KYLE   Okay, good. I'm doing an assembly at an elementary school with my friends. Oh, and I was working today. Someone did a funny hand sign at me. Then, he called me weird.

JOSEPHINE   He probably meant to say different. Different is good.

KYLE   You're weird, too.

JOSEPHINE   Why, thank you, my good sir. By the way, we're getting pizza. What kind do you want?

KYLE   (*Absentmindedly, looking back at the game.*)   Combo. The different stuff tastes good together.

JOSEPHINE   Yeah, it does, doesn't it?

SCENE 3

Josephine is sitting back in a chair alone reading. Ryan comes by and sits next to her. During the dialogue, Josephine keeps scooting away and Ryan keeps following her in his chair.

RYAN   How's your brother? I heard he got a job. I'm really surprised anyone would hire him. Doesn't he like freak out and throw temper tantrums?

JOSEPHINE   Stop, Ryan. Please go away.

RYAN   What? I'm just trying to make conversation. You do enough reading, you show off way too much anyway at class, it's not like anyone is going to like you more if you answer every question so desperately. Just dumb yourself down, ask your brother for tips.

Josephine puts down her book and turns to Ryan almost aggressively, but tries to look calm.

JOSEPHINE   Why do you even do this, Ryan? I know you have dyslexia. It's not something to be embarrassed about. Tons of people have it, and it doesn't make you any less than anyone else.

Ryan stands up very quickly, knocks over the chair, and starts backing away. He is close to, if not, yelling.

RYAN   You don't know ANYTHING. Just shut up and keep your freak brother away from me. Okay?

Ryan runs offstage and Josephine puts her face in her hands.

SCENE 4

Jamie is walking across the stage with his arms full of miscellaneous stuff. She is struggling to carry it, and Kyle is walking in from the opposite side. Jamie accidentally drops some stuff and starts picking it up.

KYLE   Do you need some help? Here …

Kyle helps pick some of the stuff up and holds it.

JAMIE   Thanks. Hey, weren't you at the assembly today?

KYLE   Um, I think so. *(He looks at a notebook of Jamie's he is holding.)* You like the Steelers?

JAMIE   Yeah! They're my favorite! You?

KYLE   Duh! Who's your favorite player? Mine's—

Ryan runs in from offstage and stands between Kyle and Jamie, yelling and standing defensively toward Kyle.

RYAN   What are you doing? Get away from her, weirdo! Just get away, okay? *(He shoves Kyle and he drops the stuff and notebook.)* Come on, Jamie, Colton's looking for you.

Ryan drags Jamie off stage and Kyle stays onstage rubbing his shoulder.

SCENE 5

Kyle is sitting onstage crying near the TV area, and Josephine runs over and sits next to him.

JOSEPHINE   Kyle? Kyle, are you okay? Did someone hurt you?

Kyle talks half whispering and muttering with few understandable words.

KYLE Your friend, Ryan … Steelers … he pushed me … Why would he push me … ?

JOSEPHINE Hey, you're fine. See? Your game's on. *(She goes to turn on the TV, but Kyle shrugs away.)* Do you want some pizza?

Kyle turns away and keeps crying. Josephine stands up and talks to herself.

JOSEPHINE Okay, I'll give you some space. Dang it, Ryan. Why would you DO that? He won't listen to me. But maybe Alyssa … Goodnight, Kyle. Um, feel better.

Josephine tries to hug Kyle, but he pushes her away. Josephine walks away and Kyle keeps crying.

SCENE 6

Josephine and Alyssa are sitting down on the ground talking.

JOSEPHINE Okay, wrap your head around this. In space, there is no gravity. That means that there is no common up or down. Someone might look completely upside down to you, but the same thing would be true for them. That someone is different than you, and you to them, but you both need oxygen.

ALYSSA And this has to do with me because …

JOSEPHINE Because everyone should be treated with respect even though they see things different.

ALYSSA English please. And not rocket scientist English, but like my English.

JOSEPHINE Okay, then … pizza. Combo pizza has all different sorts of stuff on it. They just can't help it. An olive is an olive, pepperoni is pepperoni, and so on. The sausage might say, "Wow, that mushroom looks really weird." But the mushroom is still there and can't help it. Individually, each thing tastes okay. But too much cheese and the pepper gets hurt, the pepper gets sad and leaves and the pizza can't taste as great. But if all the toppings love each other and work together, you get the pizza of awesome friendship.

Alyssa looks at Josephine funny. Alyssa gets up and starts walking away.

ALYSSA   You got me at the pizza, you lost me at the talking sausage.

Josephine gets up and almost shouts at Alyssa.

JOSEPHINE   Okay, then my brother. You guys are mocking him for things that he really can't help. And those things, if you look at him with love, make him beautiful. They make him different. *(Beat.)* When no one is different, it's boring and bland. But if you have all the differences with each other, it's exciting and really amazing. Everyone keeps talking about people loving each other. But to do that, we have to stop alienating one another. We have to make the "others" into "us." Embrace the weird. Weird is different, and different is good.

ALYSSA   You really like pizza, don't you? Okay, I'll talk to Ryan about the jokes and yesterday. But do I have to say all of that?

JOSEPHINE   Nah, he should understand with just the end.

ALYSSA   Then why did you go on with me about Kyle's space pizza?

JOSEPHINE   Ryan will understand what it's like to feel different.

Alyssa is about to leave, but she turns back around and looks at Josephine sheepishly.

ALYSSA   We were sort of making fun of you too, the other day. I'm sorry. And, you know Ryan was just scared, he didn't want to hurt Kyle.

JOSEPHINE   It's okay. I mean, I don't like it, but it's hard to change. Kyle wasn't hurt, just confused. You and Ryan will get the hang of the whole pizza idea. See you later.

They both smile and wave goodbye and leave opposite sides of the stage.

SCENE 7

Ryan, Josephine, Colton, and Alyssa are waiting for a bus.

RYAN   All I'm saying is that the bus driver's always late and it may be because he can't keep the time. He's just a senile old man.

The group looks at him accusingly. He breathes in deeply and says very precisely, as if rehearsed.

RYAN   I am sorry, that was rude. He is different than me, and different is good. We all have to be an ... Awesome Pizza of Friendship. *(Beat.)* Look, I really am sorry. I'm trying. But do I have to say all of that?

COLTON   Until you let up on the rude jokes. *(Jamie runs up to Colton from off-stage, Colton sighs in exasperation.)* Jamie! Did you miss your bus again? Why didn't you call Mom for a ride?

JAMIE   I forgot, okay? It's no big deal. I'm here now. Ooh, and so is the bus.

Everyone walks offstage like they are going to a bus, but Colton and Jamie stay behind.

JAMIE   We had an assembly the other day, kids from a special school visited. The kids were ... *(She looks back to where the other kids left for the bus.)* ... REALLY weird.

Colton pauses and shakes his head and turns to face Jamie fully.

COLTON   ... Not weird, just different. And different's good.

END OF PLAY.

Getting Past the Radar

By Ibrahim M. Sillah

Characters:

Alex Rawson – A student

Eli Fitch – Alex's best friend

Extra Student

Samuel Adams – A bully

Principal Lee – The school principal

Mr. Adams – Samuel's father

Mrs. Herb – The school secretary

Ibrahim Sillah

Sponsored by Metro Theater Company, Saint Louis, Missouri

My name is Ibrahim Sillah. I was in eigth grade at the time of the contest, and I go to Exeter Township Junior High School in Reading, Pennsylvania.

What are your hobbies and/or favorite classes?
My hobbies are playing video-games, Chess, reading, and drawing my imagination. My favorite class is Computer Apps because I'm in my element in front of a computer.

Who are your favorite writers or other influences in your writing?
Wendy Mass, Matt Myklusch, J.K. Rowling, various fan-fiction writers on the internet.

How do you think theatre (and art in general) can inspire change?
If people find a story engaging enough, I believe they can act on it.

Why did you enter the competition?
Writing is one of my strengths.

What has been your favorite theatre experience (either as artist or audience) and why?
When I was about 6, my dad wrote a speech for me to read at an event. There were a lot of big words, but I could read them perfectly. At the event, my reading was applauded, and though I don't remember what place I was in, I made podium and received a boom box.

....

Metro Theater Company

In 1973, artist Zaro Weil and educator Lynn Rubright both felt that impulse. What they made up was Metro Theater Company.* Zaro and Lynn met in the early 1970s at an improvisational theater workshop. At the time, Zaro was studying theater at Webster University, and Lynn was teaching fourth, fifth, and sixth graders in Kirkwood. Both women were interested in creative drama. To

explore their shared interest, Zaro visited Lynn's class once a week, where she led the students in activities that included movement, improvisation, music, and drama. After a year, Zaro convinced Lynn to give up classroom teaching so that together they could start a professional touring theater for young people. Zaro and Lynn gathered a diverse group of artists and played around with ideas. Young people were the inspiration and intended audience. What developed was not strictly theater, but a distinctive blend of drama, music, storytelling, and dance. School principals were invited to see the result, and they invited Zaro and Lynn to bring their performances to schools. In nearly four decades, Metro Theater Company has toured nearly 40 productions – over 30 of them original works – to 41 states, as well as to Canada, Italy, Japan, and Taiwan. Two million people across the country and around the world have seen our work. We still make theater, and we still tour, now primarily throughout the St. Louis metropolitan region, as well as outlying communities in Missouri and southern Illinois. Like Zaro and Lynn, we continue to be both artists and educators. Nurturing creative learning remains a key purpose of our work, and our educational programs have evolved considerably over the last decade to serve that purpose. Our mission thrives particularly in schools, though we are delighted to go wherever there are young people to greet us!

Originally, we were known as Metro Theater Circus; we changed our name to Metro Theater Company in 1992.

Begins in Mr. Nathan's computer applications class with main character Alex Rawson and his best friend Eli Fitch. Mr. Nathan explains how the photo-editing software they're going to use, Pixelpop, will make photo edits look more realistic.

Students murmur in interest.

ELI *(To Alex.)* Dude, imagine creating like a hybrid animal. Like a platypus-lion!

Alex chuckles.

Outside the classroom in the hallway, Samuel shoves another student out of the way.

SAMUEL MOVE! Jeez, going so slow!

ALEX *(To Eli.)* What's that guy's problem?

Eli shrugs.

After Computer Applications, Alex moves on to P.E. without Eli. As he heads to the locker room door, Samuel shoves him out of the way to get in first.

ALEX   *(Looking with shock and disgust.)* Seriously? You can't say "excuse me"?

SAMUEL   *(Looks back, daring Alex to say it again.)* What?

Alex just glares and walks in.

After the game, the boys return to the locker room. A boy gets a drink from the water fountain, but Samuel adjusts the loose faucet so the water sprays him instead.

STUDENT   Hey!

Samuel just laughs.

ALEX   *(Silently to himself.)* That's it.

At lunch, Alex tells Eli everything that happened at P.E.

ELI   That's harsh.

ALEX   Yeah. I'm thinking about reporting him.

ELI   To the principal?

ALEX   Yeah.

ELI   Dude, you'll look like a tattletale, and he'll beat you up when he finds out who ratted him out.

ALEX   But what if I do it anonymously?

ELI   Dude, this is school. You can't do anything anonymously. It's the same reason they automatically know when you're absent. Everything is traced back to you.

ALEX   I have to try. He needs to be stopped. That guy's a bully.

ELI   *(Shrugs.)* Whatever. Just remember that this is real, not some educational video on bullying.

After lunch, Alex is opening the door to the office. He is greeted by Mrs. Herb the secretary, who then asks if she can help him.

ALEX   Yeah … I … kinda want to report someone for bullying. *(Quickly.)* But I want it to be anonymous.

Mrs. Herb gives Alex a note card, explaining that he can write on it who the bully is and why he's being reported. Alex writes everything down on the note card.

ALEX   Thank you.

Mrs. Herb winks at Alex.

The next day, in between Homeroom and Computer Applications, the announcements suddenly come on and Samuel is called to the office. Samuel, acting aloof, walks to the office. When he gets there …

PRINCIPAL LEE   I'll see you in my office please.

Samuel still tries to act indifferently as he walks to Principal Lee's office, but this changes when he sees his very cross father waiting for him.

PRINCIPAL LEE   So … Samuel, we have a report saying that you've been bullying other students. Know anything about that?

SAMUEL   *(Still shocked to see his father.)* I didn't do anything!

PRINCIPAL LEE   Well it says here you've been rudely shoving students out of the way, and you used the water fountain to soak another student.

SAMUEL   I don't know anything about that.

Principal Lee looks at Samuel, not believing what he's saying, then turns to his father.

PRINCIPAL LEE   In any case, we as a district have no tolerance for bullying. I'm sorry, but if we get another report saying that Sam was bullying, I'll have no choice but to suspend him. It's district policy.

MR. ADAMS   Thank you, Principal Lee. We'll make sure Samuel here knows the consequences of his actions. *(To Sam.)* You are in serious trouble, Mister.

GETTING PAST THE RADAR BY IBRAHIM M. SILLAH

SAMUEL   I'm telling you, I didn't do anything! Who reported me?

PRINCIPAL LEE   It was anonymous. But it doesn't matter. One more report, and you're suspended.

One week later ... Alex is talking to Eli at lunch.

ALEX   Dude. I didn't get called to the office for a week. I think that report really was anonymous.

ELI   Even the principal doesn't know who reported Sam. I think you really did do it man. You got past the radar.

ALEX   I heard he's gonna get suspended next time he's reported.

ELI   Heh. Nice. Good job dude.

END OF PLAY.

AUTHOR'S NOTE

This play is meant to teach students that reporting bullying and tattling are not the same thing.

Project: Bully

By MJ Stone

Characters:

Tanner – A student

Charlie – A student

Sam – A student

Mother – Tanner's mother

Teacher

Mark (MJ) Stone

Sponsored by Yocum Institute for Arts Education, Wyomissing, Pennsylvania

School:
Grade 7, Shillington, PA,
La Salle Academy

Hobbies:
Theatre, theatre, theatre! I have created my very own theater in my basement. There my friends and I put on shows. I also perform in shows at community and regional theaters in my area.

My favorite author is Roald Dahl. I love his imagination in all of his stories. I love to let my imagination run free!

I love anything to do with theater, and when I get older I hope to work professionally behind the scenes, or in the creation process. Writing plays, I feel can help me learn more about how to create good, quality theatre.

Art is truly a magical thing. Art is the expression of the artist, and especially in theatre, the artist can give their own opinion. Art is like a persuasive essay convincing people to think one way or the other. Art can touch the heart, anger the mind and tear the eyes.

Right before writing this play, I was an actor in *Mary Poppins: The Extracalifragilistic Experience* at a regional theater in my area. In this show the kids really ran everything including lighting, sound, stage management, and production was all done by kids grades 6 through 12. This experience was truly amazing! I got to work with professional actors on a professional stage with professional lights, sets, and costumes.

Yocum Institute for Arts Education

Established in 1934 by Chester Wittell as the Wyomissing Institute of Fine Arts, the Institute opened its doors with 3 music students. Under Lila Lerch, the first managing director, the Institute grew to over 300 students and expanded its offerings to include music, dance, theatre and the visual arts instruction. An arts-based preschool and kindergarten were added and the Institute became licensed by the state.

Over the years, the Institute has forged partnerships with schools and other non-profit organizations to increase access to the arts for both arts and non-arts outcomes. In 2005 in response to a challenge grant, it launched the "Learning Through the Arts" campaign. Funds from the campaign were used to research and develop Primary Stages the Institute's signature Theatre program for children's productions and integrated arts education

Primary Stages newest venture is a partnership with Children's Theatre Company of Minneapolis formed in January 2008 when the Institute became one of 13 National sites to offer Neighborhood Bridges. Neighborhood Bridges is a program integrated into the classroom curriculum that builds critical literacy through the theatre arts.

Institute educational programs touch the lives of thousands of people each year through onsite instruction and extensive outreach programs with libraries, public and private schools, retirement communities and other not for profit organizations.

The Institute is also home to the Yocum Gallery that serves as a venue for exhibits and performances, the Berks Art Alliance and "Art Goes to School."

SCENE 1: SCHOOL HALLWAY

We open our show with a single spotlight on Charlie at his locker. Bell rings. He shuts his locker, slides down the front of it and puts his head into his hands. Tanner walks in and kicks him.

TANNER   Hey Charles! You look upset. *(Pulls out cellphone.)* Here you can use my phone to call your mommy! *(Charlie turns away from him.)* So you decided to come back after yesterday's session? *(Pause. Charlie doesn't move.)* You're making this too easy! I'm gonna throw a fist ... Boo! *(Charlie screams and runs off.)*

TANNER   Ha, Ha— *(Claps his hands together.)* —wow!

Sam walks across stage. Tanner's head follows her with awe. When Sam exits Tanner runs after her.

SAM *(Following Charlie back onstage.)* Hey I'm sorry about the whole yesterday thing. *(Pause.)* I didn't know underwear was that stretchy. *(Pause.)* I feel bad, I just watched it happen.

Tanner walks in and hides behind the locker to hear Sam comforting Charlie.

CHARLIE It's okay. I'm used to it. That Kid gives me heck every day. I don't deserve to be around a girl like you.

Charlie starts to walk off.

SAM Charlie, wait! Charlie you deserve to be around a girl that likes you. Would you wanna go get ice cream later?

CHARLIE Just leave me alone. *(Charlie runs off.)*

SAM Uggg! If it weren't for that stupid Tanner maybe he would notice me.

TANNER *(Comes out from hiding.)* Is that what you think of me?! What's so stupid about me?!

SAM Tanner! You hurt people constantly, I don't know how you can live with yourself!

Exits.

TANNER But …

Blackout.

SCENE 2: TANNER'S HOUSE

Tanner enters through a door, next to it is a wall with a picture frame on it. When he slams the door the picture frame falls and the door knob falls off.

MOTHER Tanner Oswalt, what did I tell you about shutting the door?! *(Pause.)* Shut it carefully. This house is going to fall apart! Now I'm going to have to deal with this until your father gets home!

She tries to rehang the picture but it falls again.

TANNER *(Jokingly.)* If he comes home.

MOTHER Tanner, you have to stop disrespecting your father that way ...
(She sees Tanner's disappointment in his eyes.) Oh honey, I know you don't
like him right now, but with a little bonding I think you two will become
good friends. You have to try.

TANNER How am I supposed to bond with him if he's either at the bar or wasting
away on the couch like always, and you let him do it!

MOTHER That's it, I'm going to cook dinner. You better think about what you said,
mister! Dinner will be ready at five.

She exits.

Tanner walks over to a broken chair and sits down.

TANNER Now that you've met my mother, maybe you can sympathize with me.
I've never met someone more oblivious to jerks that are single. *(He gets up and
starts pacing.)* I can't get my mind off what happened today at school. The way
that beautiful girl comforted him. *(He walks down center.)* It was ... it was ...
amazing. Why won't she do it for me? The way she talked to me as if I should be
ashamed of myself. I have a good reason for being mean to that kid! It is—uhm—
it is, ugggggggg! She knows I'm joking, right? They think I need them to feel
something! I don't need anybody. I don't need any help from anyone. I can figure
this out on my own. But how does this happen? My father always tells me how
small I am. But I go to school and everyone is so afraid of me. I don't know where
I belong. *(Pause.)* Okay, so maybe I do need someone to talk to and someone to
be friends with. Who will do this though?

Lights go dim as if were looking into his brain.

TANNER There has to be something people like about me? I've been doing
okay in school.

A spotlight appears on Teacher who is upstage.

TEACHER Tanner! What is so important about that phone that you can't pay
attention in class? You're failing my class and you don't care. Why should I care?!

TANNER   Okay well … I picked up those books for that girl yesterday.

Sam appears being knocked over throwing her books on the ground; she struggles to clean them up.

SAM   Yeah, thanks a lot buddy!

TANNER   Okay not that either. Hey! I uh, let that Charlie kid go today.

Charlie runs across the stage crying.

CHARLIE   Leave me alone!

TANNER   Well at least my mother loves me.

A spotlight appears on Mother.

MOTHER   That's it! I'm done! You think about what you said, mister!

All actors enter and form a large semi-circle around Tanner. Thought of their words starts to echo through Tanner's head. The echoes grow louder and louder and the actors close in on him as Tanner thinks.

MOTHER   *(Repetitively underscored.)*   That's it, I'm done. You think about what you said.

TEACHER   *(Repetitively underscored.)*   You're failing this class and you don't care! Why should I care?!

SAM   *(Repetitively underscored.)*   You hurt people constantly! I don't know how you can live with yourself.

CHARLIE   *(Repetitively underscored.)*   Just leave me alone!

TANNER   Come on, someone must like me. What are you trying to tell me? What am I supposed to do? How can I continue life like this? I want them to care! Not be afraid or irritated! *(Echoes continue.)* Why are these voices going through my head? *(Tries to snap himself out of it.)* Please, stop it. *(Tanner drops to the floor.)*

TANNER   AAAAAHHHHHHHHHHHHHH! Stop it, stop it, stop it! I'll do anything.

The lockers appear on stage, as Charlie did he slides down the front of it, puts his head in his arms and cries.

TANNER   This is how it must feel! I can't take it. Stop. I'll do it; I'll do something! I will … I will apologize.

Echoes stop and lights come up. It's just an empty school hallway.

TANNER   What, just happened? … I swear I was just at home. Where did all the echoes go? Have I been out for long?

Bell rings, Charlie and Sam enter having a conversation.

TANNER   Okay so how do I do this? Uggg! It's so much easier to do it, than take it away. I probably can't take it away … but I can apologize and make it better. *(He stops for a moment and thinks.)* I'm ready.

He walks upstage where Charlie and Sam are standing talking. He pokes Sam on the back.

SAM   *(Laughs at Charlie's joke. She turns around.)* What do you want? If you came to torture Charlie again I'll get a —

TANNER   *(Cutting her off.)* I want to uhm …

SAM   He's wasting our free period!

TANNER   I wanted to say that uhm … say that I didn't mean it. *(Walks away but stops himself.)* I want to say sorry. I shouldn't have done, well, everything I did.

SAM   You little— *(He lunges for him but Charlie grabs her by the arm.)*

CHARLIE   I think he means it, Sam. I think he's truly sorry.

SAM   Oh yeah? Well if you're lying, you better watch your back, buddy.

TANNER   I know, and that's why I got you this. *(Pulls out a new pair of underpants.)* Sorry about the other ones. But these are way better! They stretch double the amount!

CHARLIE   I guess it's ... okay?

SAM   So Tanner, you expect everything that happened between us to get flushed down the toilet. Charlie, you're not gonna just let it all go, are you?

CHARLIE   No Sam, I am going to let it go. He wouldn't spend money on me. He obviously means it.

SAM   So, what's your next bully method, huh? Swirlies in Fifth Period?

TANNER   No, I am actually—

CHARLIE   *(Cutting him off.)* When was the last time you went out for ice cream, Tanner?

TANNER   I don't know? Why would you ... ?

CHARLIE   Sam and I are going for ice cream. Wanna come?

TANNER   I guess that'd be great.

SAM   All right I'll give you a chance, but if you ...

CHARLIE   All right time to go!

All walk of as lights fade.

END OF PLAY.

SCRIPT 14

Can't Let Go

By Paige Wolfe

Characters:

Sorynn – Plain looking. Doesn't stand up for herself. Naïve and believes everything she's told. Depends on people to tell her what to do.

Alexandria – Confident and bold. Heavily colored eyelids. She finds a way to get what she wants and doesn't care if she hurts anyone while doing it.

Phoebe – Light and flighty in the way she talks. Petite. Sweet and kind to everyone. Against violence and fighting.

Diego – (No lines) Jock type build. Silent but strong and supportive. Listens more than he talks.

Paige Wolfe

Sponsored by Omaha Theater Company for Young People at The Rose Theatre, Omaha, Nebraska

School:
Eighth Grade, La Vista Junior High School, La Vista, Nebraska

Hobbies:
acting, writing, talking

Favorite Class:
English

Favorite Writers:
Sarah Dressen, John Green, Veronica Roth

Influences:
Everyday people and situations

Why entered competition:
Writing a play was something new and it sounded like a great opportunity to have a lot of fun

Inspire Change:
Art always has a message, big or small. It only takes one person to see it and make a change.

Favorite Theatre Experience:
Watching my play being performed from backstage!

Omaha Theater Company for Young People

The Rose Theater is committed to enriching the lives of children and families through live theater and arts education.

The Rose Theater is home to the Omaha Theater Company – the only resident, touring, professional theater company in Omaha and one of the largest in the country!

The Rose is accessible to all children. No child is ever turned away for economic reasons. "Pay-what-you-can" evenings are offered for most productions. Thousands of tickets are given to area youth-serving charities year after year.

Live performances are shared from two stages at The Rose Theater: the

CONTINUED FROM PREVIOUS PAGE

main stage and the intimate Hitchcock Theater. The national tour (when on circuit) visits roughly 50 cities each year, offering over 115 shows.

Professional actor/educators offer classes in theater, directing, musical theater, singing, dancing, and more. Children ages 4 to 18 are welcome.

The Rose has produced a number of world-premiere shows including Mufaro's Beautiful Daughters, The Wolf and Its Shadows, Where the Red Fern Grows, and The Little Engine That Could and has worked with renowned playwrights including James Still, Mark Medoff, Y York, Joe Sutton, and Robert Bly.

The Omaha Theater Company was the recipient of the prestigious Sara Spencer Artistic Achievement Award from The Alliance for Theater and Education (the primary national organization for professional children's theaters in the U.S.) in 1990.

SCENE 1

Alexandria and Diego are standing on stage holding hands. Phoebe walks across the stage. Alexandria and Diego watch her cross, before she exits Diego chases after her, leaving Alex by herself. Alex exits. The lights go down. The lights go up. Phoebe reenters walking across the other way, Diego enters after Phoebe catches up to her center stage and hands her a piece of paper. The lights go down.

Alex is standing alone, center.

ALEX I can't believe him! Ugh, I can't believe her, either. Why does she think she can just walk in here and take him away from me? We were together for three months! The record for my elementary school. I always hated when people told me Diego and I were way too young to be in love. They weren't in our relationship, they don't know anything! We loved each other, but he had no problems dumping me for the new girl, who, he knows nothing about. I hate him! But I still love him, a lot. He's completely forgotten me. We're freshmen now and he hasn't talked to me once. I've made eye contact with him, but I think he's too scared to say anything. I also blame his new girlfriend, Phoebe. What kind of name is Phoebe? It sounds like an innocent, lifeless doll. I watch them at lunch, it makes me sick. She's so kind and sweet and a little flimsy, maybe, and Diego's just strong and hot and amazing, it's just not right. And every day, I see this girl sit with them. She looks familiar. Her name's like Sophie or Sara or something, whatever. I feel sorry for her. She just sits there, watching and eating her sad school lunch. I should help her. I could use a new friend. I'm tired of the ones I have now anyways. So Sophie-Sara-what's your name, you're about to get a new best friend.

The lights go down and when they come up again, Sorynn has taken Alex's spot.

SORYNN   Phoebe's my best friend. She and I have been friends for about three years. I met her at the ice cream shop on the corner the summer before Jr. High. It was hot out and she was licking her cone and then all her ice cream melted to the ground. I was the only one who saw, we laughed about it forever and have been together ever since. Now we're freshmen and Phoebe and I are still as close as ever but she's been more focused on her boyfriend, Diego. He's nice and funny but I'm getting a little annoyed with Phoebe, because he's all she talks about. I feel like I'm a third wheel. I mean she still talks to me, just not as much as she used to. Then Alexandria, or Alex, she likes that better, started talking to me. She's in a lot of my classes. We also walk with each other from class to class, so I'm not really seeing Phoebe that much, but she's with Diego so much I doubt she actually noticed. Alex always invites me to sit with her at lunch. I sit with her but I always ask her, "Why don't you sit with us? I'd love for you to meet Phoebe." She always laughs and says "Oh, I know Phoebe." I think they know each other. Did they go to elementary school together or something? I'll ask later. There's Alex. Hey, Alex, wait up!

Alex enters. Sorynn crosses to Alex. They are now in a classroom.

ALEX   Hey, Sorynn. How was your weekend?

SORYNN   Good morning! Boring really. My brother made me—

ALEX   Wow, I'm so sorry. Call me whenever you want. My mom took me shopping, I got these new pants, do you like them? *(Without waiting for an answer.)* Really? Thanks, my mom said they make my butt look weird, whatever. Hey, does my hair look okay? When I went to straighten it this morning my flat iron wouldn't heat up so I feel like it makes my hair look wavy.

SORYNN   No, you look fine. Do I?

ALEX   *(Slightly annoyed.)* Yeah, just peachy.

End scene.

The bell rings. Phoebe is on stage putting books away. Alex and Sorynn pass her talking. Sorynn doesn't acknowledge her but Alex gives her a small glare. They exit and Phoebe is left alone, watching them exit. After they exit, Phoebe is standing center stage, blackout around her, Alex is standing on stage too, just hidden in the dark.

PHOEBE Something's up with Sorynn. She's been acting a little weird. And she's been spending a lot of time with Alex. Why would she even want to? Alex is rude to me. I wouldn't hang out with someone Sorynn didn't like. Last year I was in the bathroom and Alex walked in. I was just about to leave when she called out,

The light on Alex comes up.

ALEX *(Almost like a snarl.)* Oh, don't think you're better than me.

PHOEBE I just stopped and stood there.

ALEX Just because you and Diego have been together for two years, doesn't mean he loves you more. Honestly, I doubt he does. I mean you're not even pretty. And take it from me, he only left me 'cause he felt bad for you. I'll get him back, trust me. Nothing lasts forever.

The light over Alex goes down.

PHOEBE And then she walked out hitting my shoulder, pushing me into the wall. Why did she have to be so cruel? In sixth grade, I didn't want Diego or any other boy to like me. But when he came up to me and handed me his phone number, I thought he was sweet but nothing more than a friend. But we started talking a lot and I started to feel something for him. I didn't mean to break him and Alex up, but I liked him too much. I never meant to do that. I wish I could have talked to her. To explain that it really isn't my fault. But I don't understand what she wants with Sorynn. They've been hanging out a little too much. Sorynn has seemed to forget that we both walk to seventh hour gym together. I feel lonely. My best friend is imaginary. I need her back.

Phoebe walks off stage and the lights go down. When they come up Diego and Phoebe are sitting at their lunch table. Alex and Sorynn walk on laughing. Phoebe catches Sorynn's eye and points to their table. Sorynn shakes her head and points to Alex. They continue on across the stage, and exit. The lights go down. The lights go up and the school bell rings. Sorynn and Alex enter and walk whispering things into each other's ears. Phoebe enters a few paces behind them by herself. She stops at her locker and watches her best friend walk away. Alex and Sorynn stop at Sorynn's locker.

ALEX   Hey, are you sure Phoebe's okay with you coming to my house this Friday? I wouldn't want her to feel bad for not knowing.

SORYNN   Yeah, she'll be okay. She'll be with Diego. Usually the three of us go to that ice cream place. But we've been doing it for almost two years, so I'm sure she'll be okay.

ALEX   *(Distracted.)* Okay, great! I got to go now but I'll talk to you later, okay?

Alex exits. Phoebe crosses the stage to Sorynn who is at her locker.

SORYNN   Hey, Feebs.

PHOEBE   *(Quietly.)* Hi. We're still on this Friday, right?

SORYNN   Oh, about that. Alex invited me to her house. She and a few other people are having a little party, so I'm not sure if I'm going to make it.

PHOEBE   Can't you go late to the party? The ice cream shop has a new flavor that Diego and I want to try.

SORYNN   Then go with Diego and try it with him! You know I only get the Double Chocolate Brownie Fudge! I don't know why I have to go with you if you're just going to sit with Diego and only focus on him. A few weeks ago at lunch I was trying to tell you something and HE interrupted ME and you made me shut up! I'd much rather hang out with just you, than Diego and the love sick puppy clinging to his arm.

PHOEBE   I am not a love sick puppy! I care about you just as much as I do Diego! *(Pause.)* Please Sorynn, come, it wouldn't be the same without you.

SORYNN   *(Confidently.)* Well tough. I have plans with Alex, so I guess you're going to have to find someone else to be you're third wheel. Have fun!

Sorynn walks off.

End scene.

SCENE 3

Sorynn is at her locker; Phoebe enters and walks over to Sorynn.

PHOEBE   Hey, girl. How was the party? *(Phoebe notices Sorynn's a little upset.)* Hey, are you okay?

SORYNN   I'm fine! Why wouldn't I be? The party was amazing. I wish you were there. It would've been way more fun.

PHOEBE   *(Sarcastic.)* But you were with Alex, isn't she fun? Thought she was the best thing to ever walk this earth. Don't you praise the ground that her precious feet touch?

SORYNN   What? I don't think of her like that. She's a good friend and right now I need one because all of mine seemed to have disappeared.

PHOEBE   *(Yelling.)* Sorynn! I'm standing right in front of you! I'm your best friend! You're making me feel like that because everything you say is about how perfect Alex is or how amazing it was that Alex did this! She doesn't even like you! She's using you, can't you see that?

SORYNN   Why would she use me? She's been a better friend in the last three weeks than you have in the last three years!

PHOEBE   Why would she use you? I'll tell you why. Last year she told me nothing lasts forever, and that she was going to get Diego back. She's obviously given up on that and is now trying to take you away. She just wants to prove that she's not weak, that she's strong enough to take Diego. But all she is is weak and —

SORYNN   Shut up!

PHOEBE   *(Shocked.)* What?

SORYNN   Shut up. You know what you are Phoebe? Jealous! Jealous of the fact that Alex likes me and not you. She told me that you two went to elementary school together and she wanted to be friends with you, but all you did was take her boyfriend. So don't tell me that she's weak. You're weak! You can't even find your own boyfriend, you had to steal someone else's!

PHOEBE *(Can't believe what she's hearing.)* Oh my gosh, she's brainwashed you! *(Pause.)* Fine if you think she's so superior, go to her and become her best friend. But when she dumps you after she's tired of you, don't come crying to me. Cause I won't be there.

SORYNN Fine! *(Pause.)* I never needed you anyways; all you did was kiss up to Diego. You never once cared about me. *(Pause.)* Guess this is it. Now you can be a stupid love sick puppy without your precious third—

PHOEBE Just go, Sorynn. It's over.

SORYNN Umm, hate to break it to you but you're standing at my locker, so you can "just go."

Phoebe's lower lip trembles. She exits the stage walking fast. Sorynn takes a deep breath and closes her locker door.

End scene.

SCENE 4

Phoebe and Diego are sitting at their lunch table. Alex and Sorynn enter whispering and talking. They whisper and laugh for a few seconds until Sorynn gasps.

SORYNN Alex! That's so mean!

ALEX What? Don't you think she deserves it after lying to you?

SORYNN Well, kind of, but that's going too far.

ALEX So?

SORYNN So, even though we're fighting, she's still my friend.

ALEX *(Defensive)* No, she's not, she left you. She doesn't matter anymore. She's not going to get that hurt anyways. Come on, please help me.

SORYNN *(Deep breath.)* Okay, then. *(Sorynn crosses over and stands behind Phoebe and Diego. They don't notice her. Sorynn doesn't say anything, she just stands there, watching them talk and laugh with each other. Then, quietly to herself.)* I can't do this.

Sorynn crosses back to Alex.

ALEX What, what happened?

SORYNN Nothing. I can't do this. I'm sorry if she truly did steal your boyfriend, but it isn't my place to ruin their relationship. I won't do that to her.

ALEX Yes, you will! You'll know that what you did was best for all of us. Diego and Phoebe are so different; Diego and I are meant to be! Sorynn, you're on my side! Not hers. She stole my boyfriend! She needs to feel my pain! Sorynn, you are going to do this.

SORYNN Why? Why can't you do this? This, whatever it is, is between you and Phoebe. What you're planning to do is bullying and just wrong, and I'm not going to be a part of it. I'm sorry if you can't get over him. That's not my problem, it's yours. So Alex, if you're still going to do this you can do it by yourself.

Sorynn starts to walk away.

ALEX If you walk away you're not going to have any friends. And I can promise you, you won't have any in the future either.

Sorynn stops, slowly she turns around to face Alex.

SORYNN Well, I guess I better get to making some new ones.

ALEX Sorynn! You can't just walk away from me!

SORYNN You know, I think I will. *(Sorynn continues walking. Alex calls her name and tries to get her to come back. After she realizes it's not working she exits.)* Hey, Feebs. I'm here to apologize, I know you might not want to be my friend again, but I just don't want to think that we hate each other.

PHOEBE Sorynn, I never hated you. And I never will, but I was hurt that you didn't believe me.

SORYNN I know. It was stupid for me to do that, I don't know what was going on inside my head. Alex was telling stuff about you and she sounded so convincing, I don't …

PHOEBE I do. You chose to believe someone you just met, instead of someone who has been by your side for a long time. Why did you believe her?

SORYNN I don't know why. Alex seemed like she was telling the truth. I'm so sorry Phoebe, I promise you that I will never do that again. It was stupid and I feel so terrible inside.

PHOEBE Well, thank you for the apology. You can't have a friendship without trust. And I want to apologize for making you feel like a third wheel; I had no idea that you felt that way. I've been thinking about that and I realize I have been paying more attention to Diego than you. You're always going to be my number one.

Phoebe turns to Diego and mouths, "Sorry."

SORYNN Thank you for the apology. We're not perfect, never have been. I want to be friends again, but we both have things to work on. Like you said we can't have a friendship without trust, but we could definitely try.

PHOEBE *(Happy.)* It's worth a shot. So, Sorynn would you like to sit with me and Diego for lunch.

SORYNN I think I'll pass but maybe you and I could do something after school, we could go get ice cream? I still need to try their new flavor.

PHOEBE Oh, um, Diego and I have something going on so maybe tomorrow … wait, no, rain check, Diego. Sorynn I'd love too.

Sorynn smiles and nods at Phoebe. The lights go down.

END OF PLAY.

Acknowledgements

This anthology has been produced with help from a generous donation by Kaiser Permanente's Colorado Educational Theatre Program, which strives to inspire health-enhancing choices through the magic of live theatre. Since 1985, Kaiser Permanente has improved community health by presenting award-winning educational theatre programs as a free community service. Over 2 million people in Colorado have been inspired to make health-enhancing choices through the magic of live theatre. The programs have evolved into a series of dynamic plays, skill-building workshops and residencies which address a variety of topics for all ages. All programs are developed with the guidance of a community advisory group, health care professionals, and young people. More at etpcolorado.org.

A huge thank you to our national contest judges: Paula Donnelly, Gary Garrison, Marty Johnson, Aba S. Kumi, Tessia Philips, and Mary Hall Surface.

Thank you also to the Young Playwrights for Change Committee: Don Fleming, Stan Foote, Brian Guehring, Jeremy Kisling, and Karen Sharp.

The mission of *Young Playwrights for Change* is to produce meaningful conversations that will ripple across our nation to provoke change. Our goal is to spark conversation and discussion throughout classrooms, schools, and communities about the chosen topic. More information at tyausa.org/programs/dramatic-change.

Theatre for Young Audiences/USA (tyausa.org) is a national service organization whose mission is to promote the power of professional theatre for young audiences through excellence, collaboration, and innovation across cultural and international boundaries. Founded in 1965 as ASSITEJ/USA, TYA/USA is the only theatre organization in the United States which has the development of professional theatre for young audiences and international exchange as its primary mandates.

The American Alliance for Theatre & Education (aate.com) connects and inspires a growing collective of theatre artists, educators, and scholars committed to transforming young people and communities through the theatre arts.

Michael A. Van Kerckhove is a writer and Executive Director of Theatre for Young Audiences/USA.

Jeff Jenkins is a playwright and Senior Assistant Director, Training Director at the Northwestern University Department of Career Advancement.

Stan Foote is Artistic Director of Oregon Children's Theatre.

Mary Hall Surface is a director, playwright, producer, and teaching artist who creates theatre for family audiences, multidisciplinary collaborations, and innovative student and community engagement through the arts.

Borja Cabada is an international writer and illustrator from Spain. His artwork has been featured in several publications, and he has also worked in script development for some of the most successful studio execs in Hollywood. Waltzing Reaper, his first picture book, will be available Summer 2015. Come take a look at bonesandsmithereens.com.

Makeworks is the the independent creative practice of Larry Kozial. The studio focuses on print design, identity design, editorial design, website design, UI/UX design, website development and CMS development. Visit makeworks.co for more information.

25335123R00076

Made in the USA
San Bernardino, CA
27 October 2015